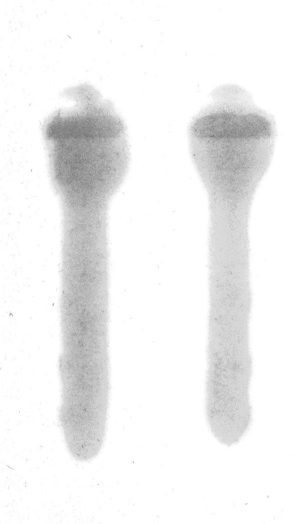

GEORGE ORWELL

The Road to 1984

Peter Lewis

Harcourt Brace Jovanovich, Publishers

New York and London

To My Mother

Library of Congress Cataloging in Publication Data

Lewis, Peter, 1928–
    George Orwell, the road to 1984.
    1. Orwell, George, 1903–1950. 2. Authors, English–
20th century—Biography. I. Title
PR 6029. R8Z726 1981
828'.91209 [b]81-6678
ISBN 0-15-135102-3   AACR2

Printed in Great Britain

First American edition

B C D E

Contents

Acknowledgements

I owe especial thanks to the late Mrs Sonia Orwell for her encouragement and guidance, for her permission to quote from her husband's works and from material in the Orwell archive at University College, London, and for reading the manuscript and making critical suggestions. She deserved her high reputation as an editor.

I am also greatly indebted to those friends and associates of George Orwell who have taken the time and trouble to discuss their memories of him with me, though they are in no way responsible for the view of him which emerges in these pages:
John Arlott, David Astor, Anne Olivier Bell (*née* Popham), Lettice Cooper, Mabel Fierz, Tosco Fyvel, Celia Goodman (*née* Paget), Jon Kimche, Arthur Koestler, V. S. Pritchett, Louis Simmons, Julian Symons, and the late Fredric Warburg.

I thank the following for permission to quote extracts from published material in copyright: Andre Deutsch Ltd and Deborah Rogers Ltd for *Enemies of Promise*, © 1938, 1948 by Cyril Connolly; Deborah Rogers Ltd and Harcourt Brace Jovanovich, Inc. for *The Evening Colonnade*, © 1973 by Cyril Connolly; William Heinemann Ltd and Holt, Rinehart & Winston, Inc. for *Infants of the Spring* by Anthony Powell; Curtis Brown Limited on behalf of the late Fredric Warburg for *All Authors Are Equal*; Hamish Hamilton Ltd and Atheneum Publishers for *Blood, Brains and Beer* by David Ogilvy; Jonathan Cape Ltd and Little, Brown & Company for *The Crystal Spirit* by George Woodcock; Martin Secker & Warburg Limited and Harcourt Brace Jovanovich, Inc. for the following works of George Orwell: *Animal Farm ; Burmese Days ; A Clergyman's Daughter ; The Collected Essays, Journalism and Letters of George Orwell*: Volumes 1–4; *Coming Up For Air ; Down and Out in Paris and London ; Homage to Catalonia ; Keep the Aspidistra Flying ; The Road to Wigan Pier ; Nineteen Eighty-Four*; copyright 1933, 1934 by George Orwell; copyright 1946, 1949 by Harcourt Brace Jovanovich, Inc.; copyright 1952, 1968, 1977 by Sonia Brownell Orwell; copyright 1961, 1962 by Sonia Pitt-Rivers; copyright 1974 by Sonia Brownell.

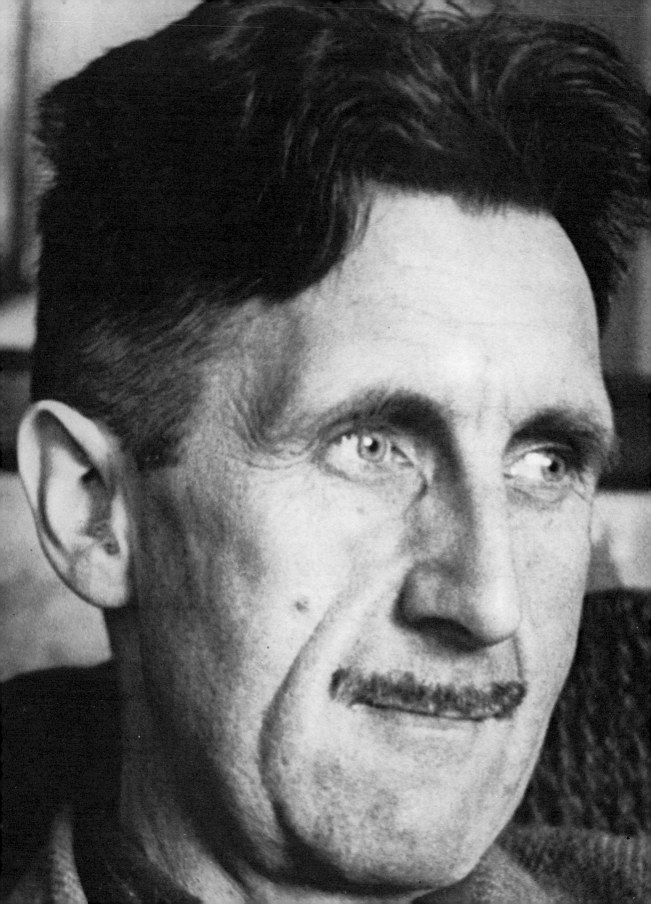

Chapter One
Profile of a Paradox

"If liberty means anything at all, it means the right to tell people what they do not want to hear." Not a familiar quotation, coming as it does from an unpublished preface written for *Animal Farm*, but the moment you read it, you detect the unmistakable tone of George Orwell's voice. The sentence is as crisp and uncompromising as a slap in the face. Plunge anywhere into Orwell's essays and one experiences the same vitalizing shock. One of many paradoxes about him is that thirty years after his death, his work is more alive than in his lifetime. No posthumous eclipse, no dated staleness has overtaken him, as they do the majority of authors. He is increasingly read, becomes more influential and remains perfectly relevant.

The combined sales of his two great books, *Animal Farm* and *Nineteen Eighty-Four*, now exceed those of any comparable post-war writer in England – indeed, in English. No one, least of all himself, would have predicted this as he lay dying of tuberculosis in January, 1950. Then, in the words of his friend Julian Symons, "he was not regarded as a classic, but as an interesting writer, who was obsessed by the menace of the Soviet Union and sometimes said things which were manifestly absurd." The obituaries were respectful but restrained. His "conspicuous honesty of mind" was contrasted with his "failures of imaginative power." *Nineteen Eighty-Four*, which had appeared only six months earlier, was discounted on many sides as the nightmare imaginings of a desperately sick man.

Thirty years later the sales of both books are well over ten million copies each in paperback. Hardback and book club editions add another million in round figures to each, and this takes no account of sales in over thirty foreign languages, including Russian with an unknown underground circulation. Very few authors sell twenty-two million copies. To do so while writing books of serious political content is a remarkable feat. Yet when Orwell died, many of his books were out of print. One had disappeared so thoroughly that a copy had to be stolen from a public library in order to copy the text for the newly-begun Collected Edition. Copies of the book he perhaps cared most about, *Homage to Catalonia*, were still lying unsold in the warehouse where they had been since publication in 1938. It had not even earned his advance royalty of £150.

Discouraging receptions were nothing new to Orwell. Most of his books had had the trauma of rejection hanging over them. His first, *Down and Out in Paris and London*, was rejected twice; his second, *Burmese Days*, was at first rejected in England and only published in America, for fear of giving offence by what it said about the British Empire. *The Road to Wigan Pier* was only issued by the Left Book Club, which commissioned it, with a long, disclaiming preface by Victor Gollancz, who also rejected *Homage to Catalonia* in principle, before a line of it had been written. Most notoriously, *Animal Farm*, the modern satire with the best claim to be classed with *Gulliver's Travels*, was rejected by three British publishers and nearly twenty American ones. Orwell was driven to making plans to publish it himself as a pamphlet.

No better proof is needed that Orwell was a prophet, ahead of his time. He told friends that until the war, his income from books and journalism averaged no more than £3 a week. When he at last found fame and the beginnings of fortune, he was too ill to benefit from it. He had only just enough strength left to write *Nineteen Eighty-Four*. His life was not only hard and discouraging but an almost continuous battle against bad

George Orwell in 1946. "His eyes were made to glitter with amusement."

The writer Julian Symons, a friend of Orwell's in his last years.

lungs – he had, as a life's companion, a disease that would win in the end. This needs to be borne in mind when considering Orwell's pessimism. He was a gloomy man, for the most part, and a solitary one. His face, in most photographs, has a certain bleak and formidable austerity which suggests a lack of *joie de vivre*. This was a misleading impression. It was a quirky, elusive but far from cheerless personality that lurked within.

The deep furrows that scored his cheeks, the hard pencil line of his moustache and his upward-bristling hair gave him the look of an ascetic. But the impression of tight-lipped endurance was cancelled out by his eyes and his smile. "His eyes were made to glitter with amusement," wrote Cyril Connolly. "A hard, almost cruel mouth until he smiled," wrote another friend, George Woodcock, while V. S. Pritchett remembered how his bleak expression would become suddenly "gentle, lazily kind and gleaming with workmanlike humour." Although he was convinced that he was unattractive to women, many women friends have testified to the opposite – "he looked at you as if inwardly he was roaring with laughter," said one. Clearly the photographs do not give us the living man.

Arthur Koestler : friend and fellow campaigner against the drift towards totalitarianism.

How gloomy was he? "Cheerfully gloomy," said his publisher, Fredric Warburg. "Like gloomy people, he could have moments of great gaiety," said his widow, Sonia Orwell, "He was much funnier, in person and in print, than people imagine." According to his friend, Arthur Koestler, "He was a pessimist and so am I, so I found it stimulating, not depressing, to be with him."

Orwell was very tall and thin, six foot three with size twelve feet. His head and hands were equally large compared with the gaunt body. His clothes hung on him. They seemed chosen for the part of a writer up from the country, leather-patched tweed and corduroy trousers which maintained always the same degree of shabbiness. At the same time he managed to give a hint of being accustomed to patronize French working men's cafés. His shirts were always dark, of khaki or navy blue, and beneath the French-style moustache would be a crumpled cigarette which he invariably rolled himself. He did not own a dark suit.

His appearance has been compared to Don Quixote's. "A frayed sahib" – Pritchett's description – seems much more apt. It conveys the style of a man used to command, someone who did not give a damn. Those who saw him in disguise as a tramp declared he was incapable of looking the part. He looked, as indeed he was, however faintly, an aristocrat, the descendant of an earl. There was a clumsiness about him too. "His sleeves always seemed to be halfway up his arms," said Symons, "You could not be with him for an hour without being aware that he thought of himself as a member of the awkward squad."

He was nearly robbed of his vocal chords by a sniper's bullet through the throat in Spain, and his voice seemed oddly thin coming out of such a big man. "Rusty-edged," said Pritchett of his voice. "A curious rasp to avoid striking a public school note," wrote his friend, Anthony Powell. He spoke monotonously, in a flat, uninflected way. Did he laugh? His friends have little memory of Orwell's laughter. David Astor, his friend and editor on the *Observer*, said he did not laugh out loud. "It was a dry laugh, almost like a cough," remembered Koestler. Connolly recalled a wheezy chuckle; Symons that his rare laughter revealed discoloured teeth. Orwell's jokes were of the kind to provoke a short, dry laugh. One of his favourites, according to Tosco Fyvel who succeeded him as literary editor on *Tribune*, was to ask devout fellow-travellers which sport Lenin and Trotsky liked best. "Shooting foxes" was the right answer.

Those who seek a simple pattern in a human life have suggested that Orwell was driven into the dramatic changes of course in his career by a "bad conscience". According to this theory, he became a dishwasher in Paris and a tramp in London in order to atone for being a policeman in Burma. The privileged Etonian compensated by seeking to share the life of unemployed miners in Wigan. The Left-winger joined not the International Brigade, but the little regarded and unpopular Marxist dissidents, the POUM, in the Spanish war.

There is some, but not enough, evidence of Orwell's feelings of guilt to justify this explanation. It is more plausible to see these events as a series of deliberate escapes he made from the predictable patterns of English life. Burma was an escape from the usual Eton–Oxbridge pattern; transition from policeman to tramp destroyed another, empire-building pattern; instead of persisting as a hard-up hanger-on in pre-war literary London, he elected to run a small village stores in Hertfordshire. The final, post-war retreat to the inaccessible Scottish island of Jura saved him from the threat of being lionised as a well-known literary man at last. There are no simple explanations for a character as contradictory and as complex as Orwell's. But it is possible that one factor in his odd career was that he always reacted against doing the conventional thing.

Orwell was not merely reserved but obsessively reticent, even for an Englishman of his background. He did not talk about his life and his friends knew that an attempt to pry might cost them his friendship. "He trusted me," said Astor, "But he never told me about himself and I never asked." "Because of the way he shut off the various parts of his life from each other, nobody knew the whole of him," said Julian Symons. "He could adopt the manner of a Burma police sergeant. It wasn't gaucheness, it was armour," said Koestler, "It was difficult, verging on impossible, for him to talk of intimate things." Orwell's vehement feelings about his preparatory school, St. Cyprian's, were unknown even to Cyril Connolly, his contemporary there, until towards the end of his life. Nothing is known of his life in Burma, little more of his struggles to become a writer. Of his wife's sudden death he hardly spoke to anyone. His inner life is known mainly through his autobiographical writing and that deals only with those parts of his life he was prepared for people to know.

The gaps have been filled by myth-making, in particular the creation of the Blair–Orwell twin personality which, it will be argued in this book, is a wholly unnecessary myth. Even if there were evidence for it, the theory is inconsistent. Sometimes it is claimed that Eric Blair, wishing to suppress the person he had been to the age of thirty, invented "George Orwell" to take his place. But at other times it is argued that George Orwell invented Eric Blair, as the subject of his autobiographical passages, which were selections from his own experience, suitably heightened. This muddle disappears if one drops the pretence that these were two halves of a split personality. They were one and the same man – a man who broke out of the mould of his upbringing in order to explore other worlds. "I ought to mention," he put at the end of his entry for a reference work, "that George Orwell is not my real name." That is all that need be said.

He was an aggressive, sometimes violent writer but mild and tolerant in his personal dealings with people. "I don't mix much in literary circles because I know from experience that once I have met and spoken to anyone I shall never again be able to show any intellectual brutality towards him, even when I feel I ought to," he wrote to Stephen Spender, whom he had classed with the "parlour Bolsheviks" until he met him. "He never *said* anything really nasty about anybody, but he could be very strong and ruthless in print," said David Astor. Intellectual brutality meant carrying on an argument without giving quarter. "If you said exactly what you thought, even about a friend, nobody should be offended."

One of those who *was* offended was one of Orwell's boyhood heroes, H. G. Wells. Wells was furious when Orwell criticized his work for what he took to be a naive belief in benevolent scientific progress and in his faith that "reasonable people" would save the human race. "I don't say that at all – read my early works, you shit," scribbled Wells. He also called Orwell "a Trotskyist with big feet." But according to Astor, when another violent protest from Wells about an Orwell review was torn up by the editor of the *Observer*, Orwell in turn was furious that it had not been preserved for its literary interest.

Another victim of his uncompromising pen was his very close friend, Arthur Koestler. "The day before he arrived to stay with us in North Wales, *Tribune* came out with his review of a play of mine – admittedly a very bad one – which was a merciless hatchet job. Not even one relenting sentence or phrase to say better luck next time. When I asked him why did he have to be so bloody about it, he said, 'Well, it's a lousy play, isn't it?' His integrity could become inhuman. The fact that he let the review appear on that very day shows his puritan ruthlessness. He was merciless towards himself. The closer you were to him, the more that harshness was carried over to you. On the other hand, he was full of sympathy for the distant masses. And there was one odd moment when he told me, 'In my bath, I think up tortures for my enemies.' I presume he meant the Stalinists." Ruthlessness towards himself, Koestler believes, was a key to Orwell's character. "He had to be hard on himself because of his illness, the enemy within. He prided himself on facing up to unpleasant facts."

Orwell was a connoisseur of the unpleasant, the unpalatable and the revolting. He not only forced himself to face them, he used his keenest descriptive powers to convey a shudder of distaste which the reader would have to share. There was, for instance, no more sensitive register of the nasty smells of life than Orwell's nose. It is thanks mostly to this alert organ that we experience the horrors of his prep school, the Paris kitchens, the London lodging houses, the Wigan tripe shops and the front line in Spain. Indeed, it could be a valid criticism that Orwell overdoes the sense of smell from a literary point of view.

But he does not stop at smells. Almost his earliest published essay is a "life study" of a judicial hanging in Burma. What haunts our memory, as it must have haunted Orwell's, is the voice of the prisoner, muffled by a bag over his head, calling on his god – "Ram! Ram! Ram! Ram!" The free hospital in Paris where Orwell was taken with severe pneumonia could not have been rendered more graphically by Goya. Orwell describes how an agonized patient was found dead in a neighbouring bed in the morning, with his head sticking out towards him. Then he notes something of interest about himself. "In the better light I had time for a good look at him. Indeed I lay on my side to look at him." After his dispassionate and harrowing description of what he saw, he adds: "There you are, then, I thought, that's what is waiting for you, twenty, thirty, forty years hence: that is how the lucky ones die." The essence of Orwell's harshness towards himself is in the word "lucky".

Perhaps the most distressing passage in *Nineteen Eighty-Four* is the study of Winston Smith's emaciated body in the mirror – its ugliness makes him weep. "The cheeks were seamed, the mouth had a drawn-in look . . . the barrel of the ribs was as narrow as a skeleton, the legs had shrunk so that the knees were thicker than the thighs." It sounds like Orwell's meticulous observation of his own body in the sanatorium – of which he used to say, "If I lose another pound, I shall be below survival weight."

Such preoccupations would make him a purely macabre writer were it not for the courage that makes them bearable. Orwell's courage had style. After the Barcelona riots, he smuggled illegal rifles for the wrong side under the eyes of the Civil Guards by walking down the street with the butt under his armpit and the barrel down his trouser leg. "The only way to move was so slowly that you didn't have to bend your knee. I saw a group of people staring at me with great interest," he noted with the verbal equivalent of his dry laugh. He tells us that to get hit by a bullet is "very interesting and I think it's worth describing it in detail". The essence of his kind of grim gaiety, which makes one feel braver simply for reading it, is contained in the incident when a man in the Fascist trenches in Spain jumped up and ran along the parapet, half dressed and holding up his trousers. Orwell, waiting in his fox-hole for a target, did not shoot. "I had come here to

V. S. Pritchett, who wrote of Orwell that he was an Englishman "who went native in his own country."

shoot at Fascists but a man who is holding up his trousers isn't a 'Fascist', he is visibly a fellow-creature, similar to yourself, and you don't feel like shooting at him." If you want a definition of gallantry, you could quote that.

Orwell never broke away entirely from the influences of his upbringing. For all his strictures on the British Empire, he admitted that it always gave him a faint feeling of sacrilege not to stand to attention during the National Anthem. "For patriotism and the military virtues no substitute has yet been found," he wrote. He was perhaps the only Left-wing thinker of his generation who would admit this. The fashion among intellectuals was either to transfer their loyalties to the Soviet Union or, like Connolly, to admire all things French. Orwell, in V. S. Pritchett's fine phrase, "went native in his own country." His originality as a patriot was that it was the English working class that he admired. His frequent appeals to "common decency" were appeals to what he saw as working class virtues – hard work, fair dealing, thrift, endurance and cheap and common pleasures which he shared himself – fishing, vegetable growing, home carpentry, strong tea, strong tobacco and dark beer. He always rolled his own cigarettes and he refused to buy lager for anyone, even women. "It's no use," said his wife, Eileen, "As a friend of his you become the kind of person who wouldn't drink lager."

He made his own list of "things I care most about". Apart from the mention of wine, it is a working class list: English cooking and beer, French red and Spanish white wine, tea, tobacco, coal fires, candlelight and comfy chairs. He wrote with passion about English puddings and on the way to make proper tea (he wanted six spoonfuls to a two-pint pot). He really was a reader of Boys' Weeklies, a collector of postcards by Donald McGill, an appreciator of "good bad books". There was a boyish streak in him he never outgrew. Fredric Warburg went on a country walk with him and, when they came to a railway line, Orwell placed a stone on the rail and sat down to wait for a train to come by. After a train had passed, he retrieved the stone sliced in half. "See?" he said.

He detested middle class stuffiness. When the management of his regular restaurant in Percy Street objected to his taking off his jacket on a hot day and hanging it over the back of his chair, Orwell's reaction was instant. He called the head waiter a "bloody Fascist" and strode out to another restaurant close by, leaving his guest, Warburg, to follow. He made a point of using the other restaurant, where jackets could be removed, in future so that the staff of the first restaurant could see him going in. His sister Avril told David Astor, after Orwell's death, that the sort of person he admired most was "a working class mother with ten children". But he was scornful of writers of the Thirties for "either pretending to be proletarians or indulging in public orgies of self-hatred because they were not proletarians." Winston Smith holds up the Proles, not too convincingly, as "the only hope" for the future. But Orwell, even in tramp's clothing, never pretended to be a Prole. He remained always aware of the gulf between him and the class he envied.

Did he actually like them? It is hard to be sure he did. His aim was to be personally as classless as possible. What he had no doubt of was his distaste for the pretensions of the English "ruling" class – upper and upper-middle. One of his last diary entries is devoted to the sound of their voices visiting his sanatorium: "What voices! A sort of over-fedness, a fatuous self-confidence, a constant bah-bahing of laughter about nothing, above all a sort of heaviness and richness combined with a fundamental ill-will . . . No wonder everyone hates us so." The "us" in that sentence is interesting.

It was easier to forget class divisions in the country, which was the only place where

A BREEZY DAY LEAVES LITTLE TO THE IMAGINATION
AT BISPHAM.

The ever-popular Donald McGill postcards which Orwell collected. In his essay **The Art of Donald McGill**, *he described them as "a sort of sub-world of smacked bottoms and scrawny mothers-in-law which is a part of western European consciousness."*

AM GLAD TO KNOW YOU ARE GIVING THE BEACH INSPECTORS SOMETHING TO INSPECT.

he felt at home. He was a devoted smallholder and naturalist. He managed to keep chickens even when living in a flat in Maida Vale. At his cottage, the former village stores at Wallington, Hertfordshire, the hens were joined by goats. Orwell preached goat-keeping to such unlikely converts as V. S. Pritchett over a good meal in Soho. He told Anthony Powell, "I don't think I could live without my lathe." By all accounts he was a clumsy carpenter, just as he was not an efficient village shopkeeper. He wrote that as long as he lived he would feel strongly about prose style and take pleasure in solid objects. He liked simple manual work and loved nearly all animals, except pigs. Until he had a child to care for, animals had to satisfy his paternal feelings.

There was a streak in Orwell which positively relished hardship. There is a letter offering his Hertfordshire cottage to a friend for the winter, on condition he looks after the animals, which reduces one gradually to helpless laughter. "You know what our cottage is like. It's bloody awful," he begins and proceeds lovingly to list its disadvantages as though to any right-minded man they would be irresistible. The kitchen floods, the chimney smokes, there is no hot water, of course, the only milk comes from the goats, which a lot of people are prejudiced against, there are no vegetables to speak of except potatoes and very few eggs as the birds are young pullets. He concludes the list with the warning not to use thick paper in the w.c., as it chokes the cesspool. On the other hand, "I dare say it would be a quiet place to work in."

His invitations to friends to visit him on Jura were weighed down with instructions for the 48-hour journey of such complexity and requiring such endurance that it is no wonder that few of them ever made it. "One is sometimes cut off from the mainland for a week or two," he wrote in anticipation of spending the winter there, "But it doesn't matter so long as you have flour in hand to make scones." Edward Lear would have enjoyed this reasoning.

Enthusiasm for adversity extended to wartime food. George Woodcock describes a meal of boiled cod and turnip tops after which Orwell declared, "I would never have thought they would go so well together." And Arthur Koestler says that at Orwell's habitual Greek restaurant "the wartime moussaka looked like a dog's vomit. But George said with relish, 'You won't get anything like this in the whole of London'." At other times he appreciated good food, but it was then patriotic, and puritanical, to enjoy bad food, a combination of motives he found irresistible. His puritanism, however, did not extend to sex, except for a strong dislike of homosexuality. He encourages his characters to enjoy sex if they can – though the cards are usually stacked against them – and elevates it, in *Nineteen Eighty-Four*, into a symbol of rebellion against the Party.

Orwell's greatest weakness as a novelist was his inability to portray love – or even to include it. The least convincing thing in *Nineteen Eighty-Four* is its most ordinary ingredient, the love story of Winston and Julia. The "love" is reduced to sexual desire, forbidden fornication and a shared belief that it is even worth getting caught to have this experience. But there is little understanding or trust between them and their mutual betrayal, when it comes, seems to be the betrayal of no very deep or valuable bond, which robs the climax of some of its tragic force.

Women were a mysteriously blind spot in Orwell's fiction – not one of them comes alive on the page – and they appear to have been something of a blind spot in his life. Apart from his mistaken belief that he was physically unattractive, several women who admired or loved him found him lacking in some essential response. "He was curiously obtuse and insensitive," said one. After the death of his first wife, he sought desperately

The American writer Jack London. Twenty-five years before Orwell he had disguised himself as a tramp in London's East End in order to write **The People of the Abyss.**

for another and proposed unsuccessfully to more than one candidate on the shortest of acquaintances. "His eye fell on me and though he knew nothing about me, he conceived that I might be the answer to his need," in the words of one of the candidates, "This struck me as a wildly unrealistic approach. I didn't have the opportunity to get to know George gradually – for me a necessary prerequisite for the sort of relationship he was suggesting." Said another candidate, "I think he loved me but I don't think he had any romantic feeling. He was really a man's man. I think that might have been an element in my not wanting to marry him."

One close woman friend of his went so far as to say that, "though he liked their company, he wasn't really interested in women." With the exception, presumably, of his

Joseph Conrad: an important influence on Orwell who was planning a major essay on the writer when he died.

wives, Orwell's love seems to have been nowhere as intense towards women as it was towards his adopted son, Richard, who was not yet five when Orwell died.

Somerset Maugham was the writer Orwell acknowledged had influenced him most by "his power of telling a story straightforwardly and without frills." If "good prose is like a window-pane", in Orwell's famous phrase, it was not such a surprising choice, although his favourite writers were Swift, Dickens and Conrad, together with a rather Victorian taste for Gissing, Samuel Butler, Charles Reade or Jack London. Orwell wrote some of the best unadorned prose in English and spent much labour on refining it. In a wartime diary he reproached himself for typing his book reviews straight out. Until then he had written everything twice over, his books three times and individual passages "as many as five or ten times". As an essayist, Orwell succeeded in writing as plainly as he spoke, while displaying a rare quality among English essayists – rude, manly vigour. Such arresting and vigorous phrases as the summary of Dickens' novels – "rotten architecture, wonderful gargoyles" – illuminate them like flashes of lightning. If he is the heir to Swift as a satirist, he is no less the heir to Hazlitt as an essayist.

He did not aim to be a purveyor of "fine writing" but to turn political writing into an art. But to him, political writing was primarily concerned with moral issues, not with dogma and doctrine, which he hated. Though always on the Left he was never of it. Looking back on the Thirties, he concluded that a writer does well to keep out of politics – but it was rare to succeed in doing so in those years. "Between 1935 and 1939," he

Somerset Maugham. Orwell admired "his power of telling a story straightforwardly and without frills."

wrote, "the Communist Party had an almost irresistible fascination for any writer under 40." Those who succumbed to it are unreadable today: Orwell is readable. He was equally rude about Auden, Spender and their movement and about the Left Book Club, for which he wrote *The Road to Wigan Pier*, and on whose startled members he lavished some of his most intemperate invective: "The mere words Socialism and Communism draw towards them with magnetic force every fruit-juice drinker, nudist, sandal-wearer, sex maniac, Quaker, Nature Cure quack, pacifist and feminist in England. . ."

Orwell was no systematic thinker but relied on intuition and gut reaction. He was suspicious of "intellectuals", had no interest in philosophy and little apparent interest in religion. Although Evelyn Waugh, who visited him not long before his death, reported that he was "very near to God", this may have been more Waugh's vision than Orwell's. Orwell's view of Waugh was that he was about as good a novelist as it was possible to be "while holding untenable opinions". Orwell's gods were such ideals as "liberty and

*Charles Dickens. Orwell had mixed feelings about the great English novelist ("rotten architecture, wonderful gargoyles") which he summed up brilliantly in his essay, **Charles Dickens**.*

justice", though he recognized that they had nothing like the power over men's behaviour as did belief in a life to come.

The nearest thing to a political programme he put forward was a proposal for scaling incomes up and down so that the highest, after tax, did not exceed the lowest by more than ten to one. To this he added vague plans for unified schooling up to the age of ten (but not after it), decolonialization and nationalization of the land, mines, railways, banks and – a sublimely impractical touch – the English accent. He supported the post-war Labour government but temperamentally he was in sympathy only with Aneurin Bevan and the *Tribune* wing. Attlee, he once noted, reminded him of a dead fish that had not yet stiffened. What were his political objectives? "That nobody should be poor," said Arthur Koestler, "And that nobody should have the power to tell anybody else what to do or to think or to feel." It is as accurate a summary as is possible to give.

He was in a profound dilemma about Socialism. To begin with, liberty demanded the right to oppose the government – but how could this comprise the right to dismantle a socialist system, once instituted? Secondly, only widespread industrialization could produce enough wealth to abolish poverty and end privilege. But, in that process, the rural England he remembered and loved was being obliterated and the common decencies of the old working class life he prized were being altered out of recognition. The trouble with every millennium that could be conceived of was that he hated the sound of it.

Having passed through his revolutionary phase, in Spain and afterwards, he found his vocation in warning his fellow men of the corruption of revolutionary ideals and the evil of totalitarian habits of thought, whether of the Right or the Left. His greatest political achievement was to see, and to make people in general see, that there was nothing to choose between Hitler and Stalin – and to do this at a time when intellectuals everywhere were bleating "Stalin good, Hitler ba-a-d", just like the sheep in *Animal Farm*. There was no subtlety about the Communist reaction to Orwell. "Slobbering with poisonous spittle, he imputes every evil to the people," said *Pravda*. "He runs shrieking into the arms of the capitalist publishers with a couple of horror comics which bring him fame and fortune," sneered the *Marxist Quarterly*. There is no quarter for a dissenter on the Left.

Orwell is read today because he asked questions to which he did not pretend there were answers. He saw why revolutions always go wrong, why plans for equality end in proving that some are more equal than others, and how, in the name of a new order, the collective will abuses its power over the individual. Because he was largely negative, destructive, pessimistic about change, he can be trusted when he offers an occasional gleam of hope, in a voice saying undramatically, "progress happens but it is slow and invariably disappointing."

One of the things Orwell bequeathed us was the adjective "Orwellian" – commonly employed, hard to define. It is a frightening word, generally applied to a society organized to crush and dehumanize the individual, sometimes signifying the alienation of that individual if he dares to rebel, like Winston Smith. Virtually all Orwell's novels have the same plot: the rebel or outsider seeking to escape from a hostile, monolithic society, attempting to make a more natural life for himself, and then being forced back into the slot assigned to him in the system. It reaches its highest development, or deepest despair, in *Nineteen Eighty-Four*. It is impossible to read it now without comparing it with the Gulag Archipelago, its camps and its psychiatric hospitals. Lubiankas everywhere resemble almost uncannily Orwell's Ministry of Love.

It was with the lonely outsider, the rebel, that Orwell naturally identified himself. Had he lived in a totalitarian society, he knew he would have been eliminated with all possible speed. He was a Solzhenitsyn without a Gulag. No one, he said, would write books unless driven by "some demon whom one can neither resist nor understand". The knowledge that he spoke for such victims and the danger that there would be many more, in many more lands, even perhaps in his beloved England, was surely Orwell's demon.

Chapter Two
Down and Out

George Orwell made a very uncertain and awkward start as a writer. His first book, *Down and Out in Paris and London*, was the fruit of five years' struggle, not just to write a book but, first, to find his subject matter and his vision of it. He found it among "the lowest of the low."

"In 1928–9 I lived in Paris and wrote short stories and novels that nobody would print (I have since destroyed them all)." It sounds like a typical false start in the life of any young man of twenty-five with literary ambitions. As he later recalled in his essay on Henry Miller, *Inside the Whale*, in the late Twenties, when the exchange rate of the franc was low, "Paris was invaded by such a swarm of artists, writers, students, dilettanti, sight-seers, debauchees and plain idlers as the world has probably never seen." It was an age of neglected genius – people who were always "going to" write the novel that will knock Proust into a cocked hat "in the rather rare moments when they are not scouting about for the next meal." Among this cavalcade wandered the future George Orwell, living in a cheap tenement hotel in the Latin Quarter, getting a few articles accepted by Paris newspapers but writing his fiction, which was what mattered to him, for steady rejection. He was discovering that a writer needs material.

All the time he could see approaching the day when his money and his life as an expatriate writer would give out. He fell ill with pneumonia in February 1929, and spent weeks in the local free hospital, the Hôpital Cochin, whose conditions were little changed from those of the nineteenth century. His description of it is probably the most horrifying single passage he ever wrote, rivalling anything in "1984": entitled *How the Poor Die*, the essay was not written until 1946, but after seventeen years his memory is so vivid that it is physically painful to read. This experience of what lay in store for the poor in hospital, where they were treated as specimens not human beings, awakened something in Orwell. When his money did run out – he says because it was stolen – in the autumn of that year, he chose not to go home, nor to ask for help or money from a favourite aunt who was living in Paris, but to plunge into the life of the really poor. He pawned his clothes and took a job in a hotel kitchen as a washer-up or *"plongeur"*.

This is the experience described in the first half of *Down and Out*. Unlike the savage account of the callousness of the hospital, it is written with youthful relish, *con brio*. It begins in the Rue du Pot de Fer where he lodged – he calls it the Rue du Coq d'Or. The patronne of the hotel opposite is out on the pavement at seven in the morning, shouting to one of her lodgers on the third floor: "How many times have I told you not to squash bugs on the wallpaper? Why can't you throw them out of the window like everyone else?" All Orwell's books begin arrestingly and this is an excellent example of his method of fixing his grip on the reader's fascinated repulsion in the first paragraph.

We are swiftly drawn into the street, "a ravine of tall, leprous houses lurching towards one another in queer attitudes, as though they had all been frozen in the act of collapse". The bugs and the guests in the hotel run by "Madame F" are introduced like fellow-lodgers. The cast includes students, prostitutes, rag-pickers and eccentrics, like the melancholy sewer-man who never spoke and who had taken to the sewers because he had been betrayed in love. It is a scene teeming with colour and eccentricity – overteeming and over-written by his later standards – and Orwell feels constrained almost to excuse himself for thus diverting us: "Poverty is what I am writing about . . .

Hôpital Cochin in Paris. Orwell was a patient there in 1929 and later recalled his experiences in the essay,
How the Poor Die.

this slum with its dirt and its queer lives, was an object-lesson in poverty." A stern reminder follows of what to expect from poverty, for he assumes that his readers do not know it at first hand any more than he did. "You thought it would be terrible: it is merely squalid and boring." Being underfed, he declares, annihilates your interest in anything but food, but it also annihilates the future and so immunizes you against worrying about it.

The most interesting symptom, however, that Orwell reports is relief, "almost pleasure", at being at last genuinely down and out. "You have thought so much about poverty – it is the thing you have feared all your life, the thing you knew would happen to you sooner or later." Poverty is a normal hazard for a rejected young writer but it is magnified into "the thing you have feared all your life." Another sentence underlines the testing quality of the experience: "You have talked so often of going to the dogs – and well, here are the dogs and you have reached them, and you can stand it." Orwell had little reason for a life-long fear of poverty but fear is one of the strongest characteristics of the book – it rises from its pages like a faint but compulsive smell. It was highly characteristic of Orwell to want to find out whether he could stand it. It was almost like proving his manhood.

19

Orwell lived at No. 6, Rue du Pot de Fer which he transformed into Rue du Coq d'Or in **Down and Out in Paris and London**.

So he reaches the first testing ground, the Hotel Lotti, situated just off the Place de la Concorde, with a grandiose entrance for the guests and, at one side, the service entrance, "a little dark doorway like a rathole", through which he was introduced by a friend. Inside the labyrinthine passages, the heat, the smells, the humming of engines, the shouting, the insults, the rush, sweat, curses and dirt were awaiting him, virgin territory, bursting with life to be got down on paper. Two things particularly fascinated him: the hierarchy of service, graded downward from the managers, cooks, waiters, to their apprentices and underlings, of which the washers-up, walking or running fifteen miles a day, were the very lowest caste; and the dirt – only a door's thickness away from the splendours of the dining room where the customers dined in elegant ignorance of it.

Orwell's relish of this paradox spurs him on to almost lyrical passages describing how cooks spit in the soup, steaks are thumbed into place with licked fingers, and how a chicken which fell down the shaft of the service lift was simply wiped with a towel and sent up again. The waiters who preened themselves in the mirror before entering the dining room a picture of cleanliness had often washed their faces in the sink where the

clean crockery was rinsing. But, he insists, this was a large, well-run hotel. A cook is an artist but his art is not cleanliness. When he moved on to a newly opened restaurant he found two rats on the table eating ham and an outside larder where food lay on the bare earth. Despite all this the restaurant was a success.

Orwell emerged from his slavery with two pieces of out-of-the-way information: pepper in the bedclothes drives out bugs; and the secret of a successful restaurant is sharp knives. Moreover, he declares that despite the exhaustion and exploitation he was often unreasonably happy. In the preface to the French edition he writes: "I would be distressed if my French readers thought I have the least animosity towards a city of which I have many happy memories."

At the halfway point in the book the narrator goes back to England on a borrowed £5 in the expectation of a job "looking after an imbecile" in the country. There he finds he has a month to wait before he can start and has nineteen shillings and sixpence on which to live. This leads him, having sold his clothes and picked up some tramp's garments, to the world of cheap and yet cheaper lodging houses in South and East London and eventually to "the Spike" or the casual ward of a workhouse, which you could not enter if you had more than eight pence in your pocket. Orwell's nose was a most acute organ and the rest of the book is pungent with its reactions. "The scene in the bathroom was extraordinarily repulsive. Fifty dirty, stark-naked men . . . I shall never forget the reek of dirty feet . . . The cells had a cold, discouraging prisonish smell – of soft soap, Jeyes fluid and latrines . . . The doors opened letting out a stale, fetid stink . . . How sweet the air does smell – even of a back street in the suburbs – after the shut-in, sub-faecal stench of the Spike."

So he follows the routine of sleepless nights in nauseating dormitories, bread and margarine, prayer meetings at which tea and buns are traded for hymns, life on the road with Paddy, the garrulous and repetitive Irishman, discoursing on the shame of his being a tramp, on begging and bad smells. One character stays in the mind out of this sorry army of derelicts shuffling along their predestined circuit, so much less alive than the ebullient denizens of the Paris kitchens: Bozo the "screever" (pavement artist) dragging a smashed foot, admiring the stars, interested in books, maintaining that poverty doesn't matter, saying defiantly "I'm a free man in here" – tapping his forehead.

One thing that may well puzzle the reader is how Orwell managed to chronicle it all in such dispassionate detail as he went along – despite the exhaustion, the hunger and the sleepless nights racked by other men's coughing. The answer to that is that he didn't. The book is not a chronological and continuous reporting of incidents as they happened but a piecing together of many separate down-and-out excursions to make one narrative. The stitching occurs in the specious-sounding bridge passage between Paris and London, in which Orwell pretends he forgot to borrow any money from his friend and was too embarrassed to go back and ask – so had to become a tramp while waiting for a job. What happened was that he went home after his Paris dish-washing, wrote it up, had his manuscript rejected because it was too short for a book, then set to work to lengthen it by gathering new material about down-and-outs in London.

Significantly, he had already begun to collect such material in the winter of 1927–8, before he went to Paris. He had already decided to get in contact with the "lowest of the low", obtained tramp's clothes, dirtied them, changed into them at a friend's house and walked into the East End to Limehouse to find a Common Lodging House which advertised "Good Beds For Single Men". He describes his initiation into the lower

Down and out on the bank of the Seine in Paris.

depths in the biographical part of *The Road to Wigan Pier*, written some eight years later. "Heavens, how I had to screw up my courage before I went in . . . Going into the dark doorway of that Common Lodging House seemed to me like going down into some dreadful, subterranean place, a sewerfull of rats, for instance." The anti-climax stays in the memory: a drunken stevedore lurches at Orwell, throws his arms round him and cries "'Ave a cup of tea, chum." "I had a cup of tea," Orwell goes on. "It was a kind of baptism. After that my fears vanished. Nobody questioned me: everybody was polite and gentle and took me utterly for granted."

Orwell changed into filthy clothes and called himself "Edward (or P.S.) Burton", but he points out that he could not disguise his accent and expected to be spotted as a "gentleman". He had a hard-luck story ready, but he seems not to have used it. When the "tramp major" in charge of one of the Spikes said, "Then you are a gentleman?", Orwell's reply was "I suppose so." As a result he got preferential treatment: a clean towel to himself and work in the kitchen – "so powerful is the word 'gentleman' in an old soldier's ear." This and subsequent low-life expeditions bore fruit in the essays he wrote on *The Spike, Hop Picking*, and *Clink*. In the last he describes how he got himself arrested for being drunk (he wanted to spend Christmas in jail) but was let out after a few hours. Both the hop-picking and the arrest for drunkenness were used later as scenes in his novels and the essay on the Spike provides two chapters of *Down and Out*.

What drove Orwell to sample life amongst the "lowest of the low", as he insists on calling them? He gave the simplest explanation in a biographical summary in 1945: "I associated with them through lack of money but later their way of life interested me for its own sake." But in 1935, in *The Road to Wigan Pier*, he gave a more complex explanation, which was so full of strange psychology that it has contributed greatly to the

Typical of the small bistros in the poor quarter of Paris that Orwell frequented in the 1920s "where you could be drunk for the equivalent of a shilling." (**Down and Out in Paris and London**)

legend of Orwell as a man tormented by having been born on what he saw as the wrong side of the class barrier:

> I was conscious of an immense weight of guilt I had to expiate . . . I wanted to submerge myself, to get right down among the oppressed, to be one of them and on their side against the tyrants . . . Failure seemed to me to be the only virtue . . . What I profoundly wanted, at that time, was to find some way of getting out of the respectable world altogether . . . Once I had been among them and accepted by them, I should have touched bottom and part of my guilt would drop from me.

In this piece of self-examination, Orwell seems to be laying his motive bare. He even admits that his belief that he could expiate guilt in this way was irrational. The guilt itself he attributes to his previous service in the police in Burma. It made him part of an oppressive system that he had come to hate with bitterness. Just what Burma had done to him will be considered in the following chapter. But the reason for Orwell's down-and-out experiments cannot be left at guilt.

It is true that he lacked money but, even in Paris when he lost his savings and took up dishwashing, he was not destitute. In England his mother and, in Paris, his favourite aunt, Nellie Limouzin, were both in the habit of helping him financially. When he came home from Burma he lived for a time at his parents' house in Southwold in Suffolk and returned there during much of the next two years. He wrote his book on being down-and-out in comparative comfort. He was down-and-out for no other reason than that he chose to be so, and even then for strictly limited periods.

There is little evidence in the book itself that Orwell submerged himself among the oppressed in order to "take their side against the tyrants." There is only a lukewarm feeling of social protest in the book. Orwell deplores the conditions of slavery in which *plongeurs* work and questions whether there is any "real" need for big hotels and smart restaurants. He discovers that a tramp tramps not because he likes it but because the casual wards may only admit a destitute man for one night at a time and the Spikes were always a day's march apart. A tramp's sufferings, from malnutrition, boredom and enforced idleness, are "entirely useless." He suggests they should be given kitchen gardens at the workhouses and made to grow their own food. He saw them as "fairly harmless parasites", who did not deserve to be so despised, but he hardly makes an impassioned appeal on their behalf and, once the book was complete, he never returned to tramping. He had got his material.

Some people have accused Orwell of "slumming". It is true that he could always stop when he wanted to, always had somewhere to go for a bath, a change and a meal and to write his notes. The longest period he spent at a time in this underworld was six weeks. But how else could he have produced his work on poverty? Certainly not by being literally destitute and without hope. He was reporting in the tradition of Henry Mayhew a century earlier, whose interviews with the denizens of the London streets make up the fascinating mosaic of *London Labour and the London Poor*. Jack London, an author whom Orwell admired, also put on disguise and tramped the East End in 1900, to produce *The People of the Abyss*. It was not so much slumming as spying.

But it is hard to equate his limited forays into the spikes and lodging houses with his claim that he was submerging himself so that part of his "guilt" should drop from him. Orwell is an uncommonly truthful writer, so one must take his word that he felt there was an element of expiation. But more than guilt, more than curiosity to see what life at

Orwell's father, Richard Walmesley Blair, at Southwold in 1937, aged 80.

the bottom was like, there was his compulsion to make himself face dirt, hunger, squalor and smells. It was will-power that kept him facing them. Orwell was a man of fastidious senses. He shows no perverse enjoyment of the dirt as is found, say, in the work of Henry Miller. But there is already a formidable gift for painful accuracy. You do not need to work in a hotel kitchen or sleep in a common lodging house, *Down and Out* makes you feel it and see it and smell it. A great reporter had found his voice.

The outcasts of society were, inevitably, romantic figures to a writer of Orwell's sensibility. "I was very happy. Here I was among 'the lowest of the low' at the bedrock of the Western world!" He had admired the swagger which the French skivvies managed to bring to their lives, and the contempt for fate's harshness exhibited by a man like Bozo, the pavement artist. The picturesque optimism of Parisian poverty was more enjoyable for author and reader alike than the hopelessness of the London poor – though the tramps were, indeed, poorer. "And down there in the squalid and, as a matter of fact, horribly boring sub-world of the tramp, I had a feeling of release, of adventure." This sentence neatly displays two sides of Orwell: his Dickensian romanticism about the underworld is coolly counterpointed by the admission that it was "as a matter of fact, horribly boring".

Down and Out in Paris and London had no easy birth. It took Orwell five years in all to experience it and to write it. When it was published at the beginning of 1933 by Victor Gollancz it had previously been rejected by two other publishers, including T. S. Eliot at Faber and Faber. It was rewritten twice, lengthened, then further revised to meet Gollancz's objections and to remove some swear words. It was an exacting apprenticeship. For part of it he stayed with his elder sister, Marjorie, near Leeds. Her husband, Humphrey Dakin, left a depressing description of Orwell going with him to visit a local working class pub. He would not join in any game or conversation but sat in a corner by himself, "looking like death", until he excused himself and went home. "I think he gave everybody the willies – and then we'd hear his typewriter half the night, tap, tap, tap." The grimness of Orwell's determination to become a writer and his anxiety about his ability to make it can be sensed in this uncomfortable scene. He reached the point where he abandoned the rejected work at the house of a friend in London, Mrs Mabel Fierz. "He left it on the floor. He told me to throw it away and keep the paper clips. He had lost all hope of getting it published," she said.

Mrs Fierz did not throw it away. She took it to the London literary agent, Leonard Moore, and bullied him into reading and accepting it. She never had a word of thanks from Orwell for having rescued the book. Leonard Moore finally persuaded Gollancz to publish it. "If you do get it accepted, please see it is published pseudonymously as I am not proud of it," wrote Orwell. He followed this up by suggesting his tramping pseudonym, P. S. Burton. "But if you don't think this sounds probable, what about Kenneth Miles, George Orwell, H. Lewis Allways? I rather favour George Orwell." In the end it was left to Gollancz to choose and to settle the title of the book (Orwell had at one point suggested "Confessions of a Dish-Washer" and "Lady Poverty"). That is how casually "George Orwell" came into being.

On these simple facts an immense psychological superstructure has been erected by some commentators to suggest that in taking a new name, George Orwell deliberately created an entirely new personality for himself, suppressing the man he had been hitherto, together with his class, his family background and his Old Etonian upbringing. The facts simply do not support such a theory. To those who knew him as Eric Blair, Orwell continued to be known as Eric, which is how he signed his letters to them. He made no sudden break at the age of thirty with his family. His younger sister, Avril, wrote that when *Down and Out* was published, the family in Southwold were rather surprised, though not shocked, at its outspokenness, and that "it almost seemed as if it had been written by a different person." This remark has been made to bear far more significance than it really invites. A book which described the hidden part of the double life which her brother had been leading would, no doubt, seem to have been written by a different person. But, she added, "it did not mean any estrangement. It is fair to say we were always a devoted family. There were never any quarrels." What sort of psychological transformation is it that leaves a man on the same terms with his family and friends as he was before?

As his literary reputation grew, naturally more and more people knew him only as George Orwell. But there is no evidence whatever that he changed into a different, self-made personality, or shunned those who knew him before his books made him famous. The name he wanted on his tombstone was Eric Blair. There was no "George Orwell" added in brackets.

Why "George Orwell"? We have the testimony of a childhood friend, Jacintha Buddicom, that he hated the name Eric because of the nauseating goody-goody hero of the "improving" Victorian school story, *Eric, or Little by Little*. He told her Eric was "not an author's name." He once wrote: "It took me nearly 30 years to work off the effects of being called Eric." But having taken a pseudonym for his book "because I am not proud of it", he wrote in another letter to his agent soon afterwards: "If it has any

Orwell (right), aged 14, with two childhood friends, Prosper and Guiniver Buddicom, during the school holidays near Henley.

kind of success, I can use it again." At that time, after so many rejections, he had little reason for confidence in himself as a writer. What he was really implying was that if this book was a failure, Eric Blair would not be saddled with it. "George Orwell" could be forgotten and, next time, he could try again under new colours. It has been suggested that "George Orwell" appealed to him because of its Englishness – the patron saint's Christian name followed by the name of an East Anglian river. Just as good a reason was the one he gave to a bookseller, Louis Simmons, that it helps an author to have a name that comes near the middle of the alphabet – and therefore near the eyeline in the centre of the fiction shelves.

To sum up, Eric Blair became known as George Orwell for purely practical reasons. Naturally, it was as George Orwell that his literary personality then developed.

This point has been laboured here because there has been so much unnecessary myth-making about Orwell as half of an almost Jekyll-and-Hyde-like split personality. He had a complex character but not a divided one. A resumé of his life up to the point where it may properly be said to have begun, with his first book published at the age of thirty, shows that Eric Blair's struggle was not to become a different person but to become a *writer*.

There is one respect in which the writer in him made a dramatic break with his natural background. He chose as his subject poverty and the psychological castration it inflicts on human beings. He did not grow up in poverty, nor was it a serious threat in his upbringing. He had to make an effort to experience it and identify with its victims. Through a succession of younger sons of younger sons he was descended from a plantation-owning great-great-grandfather who married in the eighteenth century a

Orwell's mother, Ida Blair, with the infant Eric in India.

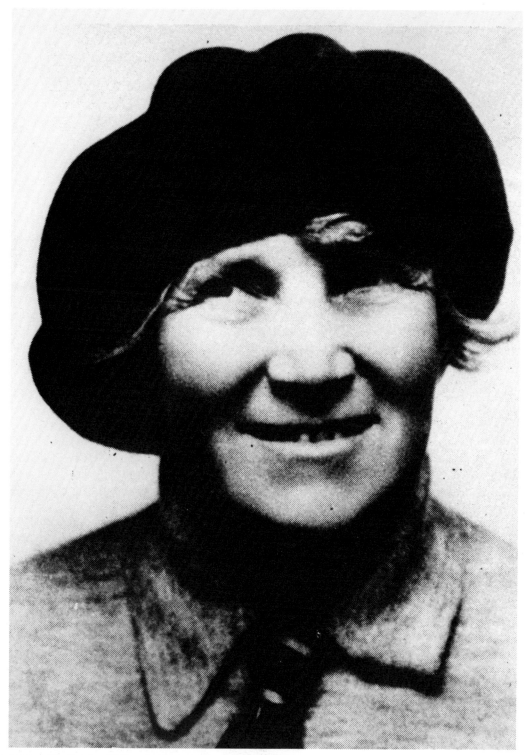

(above) *Mrs Vaughan Wilkes, the Headmaster's wife – known and feared by the boys of Orwell's preparatory school, St Cyprian's, as "Flip". "Every boy in the school hated and feared her. Yet we all fawned on her in the most abject way . . ."* (**Such, Such Were the Joys**)

St Cyprian's School at Eastbourne, in Sussex. Orwell's years there were the most miserable of his childhood.

daughter of the Earl of Westmorland, Lady Mary Fane, so he was, in fact, the great-great-great-grandson of an earl. His own hard-upness was entirely of his own choosing, in order to write. When he needed to, he got jobs teaching in private schools, then working in a bookshop.

Orwell's father, Richard Blair, was a very minor official of Empire, a Sub-Deputy Opium Agent in the Indian Civil Service dealing with the (legal) opium trade with China. His mother was the daughter of a French teak merchant in Moulmein, Burma. That is why Orwell was born in India – in Motihari, Bengal, in 1903. The following year his mother left her husband out there and went home to raise her children – Eric, an older sister, Marjorie, and in due course a younger sister, Avril. They settled in a succession of houses in Henley-on-Thames and at nearby Shiplake. Apart from leaves, his father did not come home until his retirement in 1912, when he became secretary of a golf club, an occupation interrupted by the first world war. He volunteered at the age of sixty and became the oldest subaltern in the army, looking after mules in France. It was a notably undistinguished career. Orwell scarcely saw his father in infancy and saw him in later school holidays "simply as a gruff-voiced elderly gentleman forever saying 'Don't!'" But his half-French mother, Ida Mabel Blair, *née* Limouzin, was eighteen years younger than his father. Her household was remembered by her grandchildren as cheerful, cosy and always jolly.

Orwell seems to have been born solitary. He was remembered by his sister, Avril, as "always detached and, one might almost say, impersonal" in his relations with the family. As a child, he claimed, he never felt love for any mature person except his mother, "and even her I did not trust, in the sense that shyness made me conceal my real feelings." But during the years when he was struggling to become a writer, his mother was his mainstay. Beyond writing that his early childhood "had not been altogether happy", he gave no hint of resentment towards his parents. It was his preparatory school life that he singled out for special loathing.

At the age of eight he was sent to St. Cyprian's preparatory school at Eastbourne or, in his own colourful words, "flung into a world of force and fraud and secrecy, like a goldfish into a tank full of pike." He described the experience in what is perhaps the most powerful essay he ever wrote, *Such, Such Were the Joys* – an ironic quotation from William Blake's poem about carefree childhood. He considered it too libellous to print and it did not appear in his lifetime. *Such, Such Were the Joys* is an indictment of a school conducted on the principle of a reign of terror by the headmaster ("Sambo") and especially by his wife, "Flip", whose real name was Mrs Vaughan Wilkes. This dominating woman had elevated the granting or witholding of her "favour" towards the boys into an irrational and unpredictable system of rewards and punishments that rivalled the caprice of a caliph. It was a form of psychological bullying all the more powerful for depending on the whim of a woman, at an age when a boy might expect a woman to be motherly. Sambo, who wielded the cane, was merely her executive arm.

Orwell's essay begins with a description of a beating for wetting the bed followed by another beating for saying, in Flip's hearing, that the first beating had not hurt. The second beating broke Sambo's riding crop but it was not pain, Orwell says, that reduced him to tears but "a sense of desolate loneliness and helplessness, of being locked up not only in a hostile world but in a world of good and evil where the rules were such that it was actually not possible for me to keep them. . . . This was the great, abiding lesson of my boyhood: that I was in a world where it was *not possible* for me to be good."

Part of the reason it was not possible was that the rich boys were favoured and never caned, whereas he was picked on as a "poor" boy who had been taken at reduced fees – in the hope that he would win a scholarship and bring credit on the school – and was reminded of this publicly in all sorts of humiliating ways. For instance, he did not get his own cricket bat because "your parents wouldn't be able to afford it" (in fact they had sent the money). He was only given twopence, instead of the usual threepence a week pocket money. He was goaded into cramming for his exams with such remarks as Flip's "You know your people aren't rich, don't you? How are they to send you to a public school if you don't win a scholarship? And do you think it's quite fair to *us*, the way you're behaving? After all we've done for you?" The alternatives were starkly presented: either

An illustration from the Victorian story **Eric, or Little by Little**. *Orwell disliked being called Eric because of its association with the book.*

Cyril Connolly, a friend and fellow pupil of Orwell's at St Cyprian's – photographed by another illustrious pupil, Cecil Beaton.

a scholarship or a life as "a little office boy on £40 a year." Orwell says he believed this would indeed be his fate. In the event he won two scholarships, one to Wellington and the other to Eton. But he was not grateful to Flip and Sambo for all they had done for him.

"All through my boyhood I had a profound conviction that I was no good." This sense of shame, haunted his schooldays and was provoked above all by the accusing eyes and wheedling manner of Mrs Wilkes. "It was very difficult to look her in the face without feeling guilty, even at moments when one was not guilty of anything in particular." Orwell always exhibited a lively sense of guilt and the regime of St. Cyprian's was clearly designed to develop it to excess. Yet, he admitted with disgust, "whenever one had the chance to suck up, one did suck up and at the first smile one's hatred turned into a sort of cringing love . . . as helpless as a snake before the snake charmer." Inside, however, there was no cringing. In the incorruptible inner self at the middle of one's heart, "one's only true feeling was hatred."

Learning to hate is a form of refusing to conform and Orwell learned it at St. Cyprian's. It may well have been a more important development of his character than consciousness of failure of which he makes so much. He says he did not question the prevailing beliefs of the school because he knew no others. The rich, the strong, the elegant could not be in the wrong. And by their assumptions he was damned. "I had no money, I was weak, I was ugly, I was unpopular, I had a chronic cough, I was cowardly, I smelt . . . The conviction that it was *not possible* for me to be a success went deep enough to influence my actions far into adult life." And finally, upon leaving for public school, he knew that "in a world where the prime necessities were money, titled relatives, athleticism, tailor-made clothes, neatly brushed hair, a charming smile, I was no good

. . . Failure, failure, failure – that was by far the deepest conviction that I carried away.''

The essay is a brilliant piece of destructive propaganda. It must therefore be suspect as a reliable key to understanding Orwell's psychology. It is possibly unfair to the school. Cyril Connolly, writing of St. Cyprian's in *Enemies of Promise* painted a less horrific picture of a place where "character" was encouraged as a basis on which its pupils would one day administer the British Empire. He confirms Flip's snake-charming ability to manipulate little boys into an Elizabeth-and-Essex relationship of Queen and favourite. But he writes of Orwell: "He saw through St. Cyprian's, despised Sambo and hated Flip . . . alone among the boys he thought for himself and rejected not only St. Cyprian's but the war, the Empire, Kipling, Sussex and Character." If this is accurate it was in his tender years at St. Cyprian's that Orwell learned not so much that he was a failure (after all, he had the scholarships to prove otherwise) but that he was an outsider and that he could stand it. Incidentally, it is interesting to learn from Connolly that Orwell's reduced fees remained a total secret from his fellow pupils.

In later life, Connolly's attitude to the school softened on re-reading some of his reports and letters home. Mrs Wilkes, he concluded, used too much violence and emotional blackmail but was "warm-hearted and an inspired teacher." Hindsight sometimes lends enchantment to the view but it did not do so in the case of another pupil, David Ogilvy, the founder of a well-known advertising agency, who was there about ten years later. He called Mrs Wilkes "a satanic woman" who played games of emotional cat-and-mouse against every boy at the school "like a chess master". "Boys who were lucky enough to have rich or aristocratic fathers were always in favour but boys whose fathers, like mine, were neither were always out of favour. I lived in a black cloud of rejection." In his memoir, *Blood, Brains and Beer*, Ogilvy goes on to accuse Mrs Wilkes of making such exorbitant profits out of starving the ninety boys in the school that she was able to rent grouse moors in Scotland and send her sons to Eton – a stroke that Orwell's portrait of her lacked.

Ogilvy's venom confirms Orwell's feelings rather than Connolly's. But what really matters is not what other pupils thought of the school but how it remained in Orwell's memory – and to him it was Dickens' Blacking Factory or Kipling's House of Desolation. "I wonder how you can write about St. Cyprian's," he wrote to Connolly in 1938, "It's all an awful nightmare to me and sometimes I think I can still taste the porridge (out of those pewter bowls, do you remember?)" They were the bowls whose dried porridge encrusted under the rim he was to describe so unforgettably. And then, in the letter, his feelings flash out across the gulf of years: "And do you remember my bringing back to school a copy of Compton Mackenzie's *Sinister Street* and that filthy old sow, Mrs Wilkes, found out and there was a fearful row?" Filthy old sow she still was to him, with a resentment unsoftened by the passage of twenty-five years.

After a term at Wellington, awaiting a vacancy in the limited number of King's Scholars at Eton, he changed schools. He never wrote of his time in College at Eton, except to say that he did no work and did not feel Eton was a formative influence on him. The school had one great virtue, he wrote years later – "a tolerant and civilized atmosphere which gives each boy a fair chance of developing his own individuality." He seems to have used this opportunity to avoid distinction, except in the Wall Game. Photographs of him at school show a look of faint amusement which tallies with Connolly's memory of him being "extreme and aloof". The boys of Orwell's year reacted against the traditions of savagery in the form of bullying, beating and fagging,

Orwell at Eton : Aged 16, outside the Fives Court.

Going swimming with a friend, Ralph Cazalet.

A. S. F. Gow – Orwell's first tutor at Eton, later to gain a distinguished reputation as a classicist at Cambridge.

and formed, said Connolly, "an oasis of enlightenment among the reactionaries."

Connolly's theory of "permanent adolescence" – that public schoolboys in England are dominated by their school experience for the rest of their lives – provoked Orwell's scorn. But in a way he half agreed. "Cultured middle-class life has reached a depth of softness at which a public school education – five years in a lukewarm bath of snobbery – can actually be looked back upon as an eventful period." Continental writers, he maintained, at least knew the meaning of more important things such as hunger and hardship, war and persecution. But if Eton left little mark, the psychological violence of St. Cyprian's and Mrs Wilkes must have done so. The fascinating but unanswerable question is how much?

In 1921 came a surprising transition from Eton to the Indian Imperial Police. Orwell offered no reason why he did not take the usual path (for a scholar) to university. After all his scholarship cramming at St. Cyprian's he had "slacked off" at Eton. His tutor, Andrew Gow, told his father that he had not the faintest hope of getting a university scholarship, without which Oxford or Cambridge were out of the question financially. He may not have been interested in going to either of them. He may have felt the call of the East, where his family roots were.

He sailed for Burma, after some preliminary examinations, in October, 1922, aged nineteen. In spite of his apparent acquiescence in a career in a colonial police force, he did let slip in his key essay, *Why I Write*, that he must have known it was all a mistake. He admitted there that he had known from the age of five or six that he should be a writer. "Between 17 and 24, I tried to abandon this idea, but with the consciousness that I was outraging my true nature." So far he had published two patriotic poems, on the outbreak of the Great War and on the death of Lord Kitchener, in his local paper, the *Henley Standard*. He wanted to write enormous naturalistic novels, full of purple passages. Throughout his school years, he says, he had felt compelled to make up in his head a running story about himself, with meticulous descriptions of his everyday experiences as they happened. "I knew I had a facility with words and a power of facing unpleasant facts . . . I felt this created a sort of private world in which I could get my own back for my failure in everyday life." This private world he now took with him to Mandalay.

Chapter Three
The Thirties

If public school had been, for Orwell, "five years in a lukewarm bath of snobbery", the Burma police was five years in a steam-bath of self-doubt. He served there from 1922–27 as an assistant superintendent of police in Myaungmya, Upper Burma, where he took charge of a district headquarters with between thirty and fifty men, and later at five other stations including Moulmein in steamy Lower Burma. Between them, these stations gave him the experiences on which he based not only his first and most satisfactory novel, *Burmese Days*, but also the essays, *A Hanging and Shooting an Elephant*, two of his most masterly pieces of physical description.

At the Police Training School in Mandalay, Burma, 1923. Orwell is third from the left in the back row.

Later, Orwell dismissed his years in Burma as "five boring years within the sound of bugles" which made him hate imperialism. Writing nearer to the time he was there, he betrayed feelings of bitter outrage at the role forced on him as a representative of imperialism, mixed up with a grudging respect, even pride, in the traditions of the service. All this is wonderfully compressed into *Shooting an Elephant* which he wrote in 1936, three years after *Burmese Days* was finished.

It begins with one of Orwell's arresting sentences "In Moulmein, in Lower Burma, I was hated by large numbers of people" – and goes on to describe how he was already secretly on the side of those people. He had already decided that imperialism was an evil thing and "the sooner I chucked up my job and got out the better." And yet he had little love for the Burmese, who baited and laughed at him and shouted insults whenever it was safe to do so, especially for the Buddhist priests who stood on street corners and jeered at Europeans. "I was stuck between my hatred of the empire I served and my rage against the evil-spirited little beasts who tried to make my job impossible. With one part of my mind I thought of the British Raj as an unbreakable tyranny . . . with another part I thought that the greatest joy in the world would be to drive a bayonet into a Buddhist priest's guts. Feelings like these are the normal by-products of imperialism."

There is enough to Orwell's personal discredit in this account to make one accept it as the painful truth. Christopher Hollis, a fellow Etonian who visited him in Rangoon in 1925, remembered "he was at pains to be the imperial policeman, explaining that these theories about no punishment and no beating were all very well at public schools but that they did not work with Burmese." Yet, when Orwell tried to explain what had given him his guilt at doing "the dirty work of Empire", he listed "the stinking cages of the lock-ups, the grey cowed faces of the long-term convicts, the scarred buttocks of the men who had been flogged with bamboos." In the autobiographical section of *The Road to Wigan Pier* he added, "I watched a man hanged once; it seemed to me worse than a thousand murders. I never went into a jail without feeling that my place was on the other side of the bars." There is a characteristic extremism of language for rhetorical effect. Elsewhere he admits to having struck and kicked Burmese.

In five years as a policeman carrying the responsibility for law and order in a large district, Orwell learned what it is like to govern unwilling subjects. He must have witnessed and perhaps had to order flogging and bullying, if not torture, as is done in the interrogation in *Burmese Days*. It was in this contradictory state of mind that he shot the elephant, unwillingly, in front of a large, expectant crowd, simply in order not to look a fool. "And it was at this moment as I stood there with the rifle in my hands that I first grasped the hollowness, the futility of the white man's dominion in the East . . . In reality I was only an absurd puppet, pushed to and fro by the will of those yellow faces behind . . . A sahib has got to act like a sahib . . . And my whole life, every white man's life in the East, was one long struggle not to be laughed at."

In his writings about Burma, even more than in his down-and-out descriptions of squalor, Orwell shows what an intensely physical writer he is. He has the power to make one feel literally squeamish, both at the prolonged and agonizing death of the elephant, which Orwell's rifle could not bring to an end, and at the grinning corpse of the Indian whom the elephant had ground into the earth with his foot. He fixes a telling physical detail in your mind to convey his emotion without stating it. At the moment the first bullet hits the browsing animal "he neither stirred nor fell, but every line of his body had altered. He looked suddenly stricken, shrunken, immensely old . . . one could have imagined him thousands of years old."

In the case of the man who is being led to the gallows in *A Hanging*, the moment comes when he steps lightly aside to avoid a puddle on the path. "When I saw the prisoner step aside to avoid the puddle I saw the mystery, the unspeakable wrongness of cutting a life short when it is in full tide. This man was not dying, he was alive just as we were alive . . . His brain still reasoned – even about puddles." It is the same with man and elephant. The man, absurdly, avoids dirtying his feet, although he will be dead within a minute or two; the elephant is beating a bunch of grass against his knees at the moment he is shot, unaware that he will never taste it. He is to be cut short that instant by "a mysterious and terrible change." In depicting those moments Orwell discovered his own peculiar power to deliver the shock of truth, and make the reader wince at it.

Burmese Days was the first novel Orwell completed. He began it as soon as *Down and Out* was finished in 1931 and completed it in late 1933. It was not his first novel published in England because Gollancz initially rejected it for fear of libel – so it was first

On a road in Mandalay about the time that Orwell was stationed there.

published in America. It portrayed the small British ex-patriate community of a district in Upper Burma as selfish, greedy and ignorant exploiters of the native Burmese, whom they despised as if they were virtually animals. "In my young days, when one's butler was disrespectful, one sent him along to the jail with a chit saying 'Please give the bearer fifteen lashes'. Those days are gone forever, I am afraid." Such was the small talk of the European Club.

The hero of the novel – victim would be a better word – is an English timber merchant of thirty-five, named Flory. In many ways Flory is a projection of Orwell's opinions. He secretly despises the exceptionally nasty little band of *pukka sahibs*, who live by the maxims of "Keeping up our prestige", "The firm hand (without the velvet glove)", and "We white men must hang together." He sees the British Raj as organized robbery of the country's resources, disguised by paternalistic humbug about the white man's burden. He appreciates the country and the native customs. As with E. M. Forster's hero of *A Passage to India* (published when Orwell was out in Burma), Flory's only real friend is an Indian doctor, a man who naively admires the British for "your superiority to we Orientals." But he funks proposing his friend for membership of the European club, whose nigger-hating members he describes as "dull, boozing, witless porkers" . . . whereas Forster's hero defended his friend against the attacks of an entire white club. There are no white heroes in Orwell's Burma. But there are no Burmese heroes either: the chief villain is the bribing, blackmailing, betraying magistrate, U Po Kyin. To old India Hands, such as the Blairs, it must have been a shocking book. Even

Malcolm Muggeridge was moved to reproof: "There is much more to be said for British rule than Orwell says."

Flory is so starved of sympathetic or intelligent company that he pursues Elizabeth, the first husband-hunting girl who comes out from England, not noticing the fact that she is just as shallow, prejudiced and intolerant as any of the cocktail-drinking memsahibs at the club. Their only common interest is found in the excitement of a leopard hunt, which typically brings out the best of Orwell's powers of description of animals, jungle and physical skill. There are many brilliant passages which show how acutely he registered and responded to the landscapes and people of Burma, where his mother's family had spent their lives. He said himself, "the descriptions of scenery aren't bad."

Flory's drinking bouts, treatment of his Burmese mistress and moral cowardice in deserting his friend are not, as far as we know, typical of Orwell's behaviour in Burma. But he obviously shared some of Flory's feelings of shame and disgust symbolized by his birthmark, a disfiguring blotch like a mark of Cain, which makes him continually turn one side of his face away and undermines all his actions.

"All over India there are Englishmen who secretly loathe the system of which they are part, and just occasionally, when they are in the right company, their hidden bitterness overflows." In *Wigan Pier* Orwell describes a night he spent talking on a train to a man in the Educational Service, damning the British Empire, speaking forbidden things, "and in the haggard morning light when the train crawled into Mandalay, we parted as guiltily as any adulterous couple." He did not put any such understanding confidant among the white characters of *Burmese Days*. Flory is condemned to keep his conscience to himself, as Orwell must have concealed his from his superiors. "I was young and ill-educated and had to think out my problems in the utter silence that is imposed on every Englishman in the East," he recalled.

When he came home on leave in the summer of 1927, he decided he could no longer bear his silent acquiescence in a job he did not like or approve. "One sniff of English air" was enough to decide him never to return to Burma. But when he told his family that he would resign, he did not apparently say a word about the guilt and hatred he made so much of later. He told them he was determined to write and would make his own way. His sister Avril remembered him being especially remote on his return from Burma. He had grown a moustache lining his upper lip, a curious concession to militarism that he retained all his life. He threw cigarette ends on the floor as if he expected servants to clear up after him ... which of course, they had done, just as he had been dressed and undressed by his Burmese servant. None of this seems to have upset Orwell noticeably at the time. He later admitted to remembering "subordinates I had bullied and aged peasants I had snubbed, servants and coolies I had hit with my fist in moments of rage" – but he also made allowances. "Living and working among Orientals," he wrote, "would try the patience of a saint."

Burma changed Orwell permanently by putting him on the side of the underdog everywhere. But this never blinded him, as it blinds so many of the Left, to the virtues, such as they are, of the oppressors, or top dogs. Orwell's essay on Kipling, written in 1946, distils this dual attitude which remained with him for life. After declaring that Kipling's jingo imperialism is morally insensitive, aesthetically disgusting and cannot be accepted or even forgiven by any civilized person, he goes on to excuse Kipling for being a "vulgar flag-waver". He did not realize that "an empire is primarily a money-making

Rudyard Kipling. "Few people . . . have said bitterer things about England than this gutter patriot" wrote Orwell in an essay in which he confessed his ambivalent attitude towards Kipling.

concern" and that "we all live by robbing Asiatic coolies" – our standard of living depends on the robbery continuing. Kipling admired the administrators, soldiers and engineers of British India because he preferred "the active man to the sensitive man" and the nineteenth-century Anglo-Indian empire-builders "were at any rate people who did things." They built India a railway system, for example. They could have achieved nothing if they had had the "enlightened" outlook of E. M. Forster. One thing possessed by the official class with whom Kipling identified was a sense of responsibility. Besides, Kipling did not really resemble the empire-builders but was in many ways an outsider, a journalist, whom they suspected of having Asiatic blood and mixing with the "wrong" people.

Immediately one can sense Orwell's sympathies being aroused. "Few people have said bitterer things about England than this gutter patriot." Orwell was the first critic to point out that a poem like *Recessional* was a denunciation of vainglorious "dominion over palm and pine". On top of which Kipling was a "good bad poet", horribly vulgar on occasion but capable at the same time of giving genuine poetic pleasure, for example in the poem *Mandalay*. Kipling "sold out emotionally to the British governing class", who were not what he imagined, but at least he tried to imagine what action and responsibility were like.

This extraordinary conflict of feelings and instincts brings us close to the centre of Orwell. He confessed on another occasion: "I worshipped Kipling at 13, loathed him at

17, enjoyed him at 20, despised him at 25 and now again (1936) I rather admire him." You can sense his own Kiplingesque sympathy with men of action and responsibility, who hold the fort and get the railways built, struggling with his fierce disapproval of the "monstrous intrusion of one race ruling another and making money out of it." It is hard to say which feeling wins. It is almost as though Orwell, like Kipling, imagined an ideal empire run by men of such high principle that it would be acceptable morally.

Orwell's early novels, *A Clergyman's Daughter* and *Keep the Aspidistra Flying* continue in the form of invented stories the observations he first wrote as straightforward reportage in *Down and Out in Paris and London*. Both of them deal with rather superior middle-class characters who drop out, discovering the seamy side of poverty, and then return to the way of life that has shaped them. The clergyman's daughter Dorothy, who leads a life of harassed, pinched gentility running her father's parish errands, reaches the down-and-out world by way of an unconvincing loss of memory. She suddenly finds herself tramping ("on the beach", the other derelicts call it), and tramps into Kent to go hop-picking, as Orwell had done in 1931. There is an idyllic picture of the pickers singing in the fields in the smell of hops and woodsmoke. Despite exhaustion and low wages, "You were happy, with an unreasonable happiness. It was stupid work, mechanical, exhausting and every day more painful to the hands, and yet you never wearied of it . . . you had the feeling you could go on picking forever and forever."

Then follows for Dorothy a night spent in Trafalgar Square, huddled together for warmth with other homeless people, cocooned in newspaper bills to keep out the cutting wind. This, too, was described from experience. Orwell goes rather self-consciously "modern", writing the scene in dialogue and stage directions, as if it were a scene in a play. He later claimed this was the only chapter he was pleased with. Nevertheless he has to go back into prose to make his point – that sleeplessness and exposure blur your perceptions until the world grows as unreal and vague as a dream. Dorothy, again like Orwell, continues her odyssey by teaching in a dismal private school near London, which is a racket for extracting fees and imparting no education in return. (Orwell taught

Richard Rees, painter and critic. Editor of **The Adelphi** *magazine and a close friend and patron of Orwell.*

at a private school at Hayes in 1932.) Eventually she is restored to the miseries of life in the vicarage, only by now with no faith, only habit, to sustain her.

Orwell's comments on his own work were brutal. *A Clergyman's Daughter*, he said succinctly, was "tripe" and "was written simply as an exercise and I oughtn't to have published it, but I was desperate for money." The same applied, he said, to *Keep the Aspidistra Flying*. By the time he wrote that (1935), he had moved to London permanently and was working as an assistant in "Booklover's Corner", a bookshop on the corner of South End Green, just below the lower edge of Hampstead Heath. He had a room over the bookshop where he wrote poetry and book reviews for the magazine *The Adelphi* (for a short while called *The New Adelphi*), thanks largely to his friendship with Sir Richard Rees, who edited and helped finance it. All this comes into the novel, whose hero, Gordon Comstock, hates working in just such a bookshop, toils unsuccessfully at writing poetry, and has a rich patron with a literary magazine, from whom he is too proud to ask for straightforward financial help. But the real subject of the novel is money and Gordon's attempt to reject the way of life based on money. He becomes a "drop-out", partly out of disgust with advertising and the fear of the sack, partly because he believes he is destined to be a poet – he has had one slim volume mildly approved by the *Times Literary Supplement* and tinkers obsessively with a long, depressing poem called "London Observed".

Gordon is an irritating character because he repeats his self-pitying obsession with his own poverty like a gramophone record. "Poverty is spiritual halitosis." Because of it, he claims, he is shunned by his friends, his work is rejected by snobbish poetry magazines and his girl won't sleep with him. There was nowhere to invite her to go – landladies didn't allow women in – "only the streets and the parks where it is always cold. It is not easy to make love in a cold climate when you have no money." So he goes on a bender with a £10 royalty cheque and is arrested and charged with drunkenness – Orwell's contrived experience, first recorded in the essay entitled *Clink*.

After that Gordon sinks to the bottom, living in squalid lodgings, working in a squalid bookshop that sells only cheap trash, a process of degradation described with a sort of romantic longing that Orwell was to use of his own down-and-out days: "Under ground. Down in the safe soft womb of earth where there is no getting of jobs or losing of jobs, no relatives or friends to plague you, no hope, fear, ambition, honour, duty – that was where he wished to be." There is an almost moralizing Victorian satisfaction in the passages that depict the degradation and wretchedness to which Gordon surrenders, appalling his rich friend Ravelston: "Dash it, Gordon was a gentleman!" The thought of Gordon, who was of gentle birth, lurking in that vile place and that menial job "worried him more than ten thousand unemployed in Middlesbrough." It is the best scene in the book. Orwell can sympathize with both men, the outraged class instincts of Ravelston, which he shared, and Gordon's amusement at outraging them, which he also shared. He is writing about two sides of his own character.

Gordon is finally won back to conformity by his girl friend, Rosemary. After the embarrassing failure of his first open-air seduction of her – when Gordon's mind is obsessed about the eight pence which is all he has left in his pocket – Rosemary takes pity on him in his down-and-out lodging, gets pregnant and thereby tempts him back to the career in advertising that he had spurned so contemptuously as a would-be poet. He puts his never-finished poem down a drain and rejoins the respectable ranks of the human race, who live by the money-code and keep the aspidistra flying as the symbol of their aspirations to make good.

Sardonic as it is, this is the least satisfactory, most confused part of a confused book. One feels that for one of the few times in his life, Orwell refused to call a sell-out a sell-out, in order to provide an up-beat ending to a sour novel. But he never succeeds in making Gordon Comstock worthy of sympathy. Apart from his self-pity, what did the man prove by rebelling against convention for a few months? Only what little talent and what little stamina he had as a would-be poet.

"Apart from projections of himself, the characters of his novels do not live as persons," wrote Anthony Powell in a widely-shared judgement of Orwell as novelist. But Gordon is only partially another of Orwell's projections of himself. He did take direct from life the boredom of the bookshop, the dingy frugality of life in cheap rooms, the embarrassments of weekend sorties with girls into the country which he couldn't quite afford. According to Ruth Pitter, who was one of those he took out, "It was terrible to him to let a woman pay." "Have you ever had a woman in the park?" he demanded of Anthony Powell, "I was forced to. Nowhere else to go." He was gratified to get letters from a number of young men confirming the truth of his description of the miseries of such weekend wooing on insufficient funds.

But Orwell was never a whining drop-out like Comstock. Their only resemblance was in the lack of initial talent and success. The poem with which Gordon is tinkering throughout the novel, until he throws it down the drain, was actually published by Orwell over his new *nom de plume* in *The Adelphi* in 1935. It is a pretty bad poem. So were the dozen or so poems he had previously contributed to *The Adelphi* as "Eric Blair". Orwell's very virtue as a writer of colloquial prose made him clumsy and unmusical in verse. Yet it seems that much of these early years was spent in struggling to write poetry. "I don't think any of his friends believed he would ever write well," said Ruth Pitter, the poet who befriended him, "We used to laugh till we cried at some of the bits he showed us." Orwell's secret fear that he is never going to make a poet – and

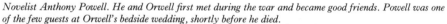

Novelist Anthony Powell. He and Orwell first met during the war and became good friends. Powell was one of the few guests at Orwell's bedside wedding, shortly before he died.

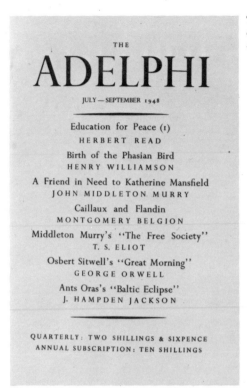

THE

ADELPHI

JULY — SEPTEMBER 1948

Education for Peace (1)
HERBERT READ

Birth of the Phasian Bird
HENRY WILLIAMSON

A Friend in Need to Katherine Mansfield
JOHN MIDDLETON MURRY

Caillaux and Flandin
MONTGOMERY BELGION

Middleton Murry's "The Free Society"
T. S. ELIOT

Osbert Sitwell's "Great Morning"
GEORGE ORWELL

Ants Oras's "Baltic Eclipse"
J. HAMPDEN JACKSON

QUARTERLY: TWO SHILLINGS & SIXPENCE
ANNUAL SUBSCRIPTION: TEN SHILLINGS

The Adelphi *published many of Orwell's book reviews and some of his rare poems, the latter under the name Eric Blair.*

possibly not a novelist either, in view of *A Clergyman's Daughter* – comes out in Gordon's bitterness in the bookshop at the sight of "snooty, 'cultured' kinds of books . . . criticism and belles lettres that those moneyed young beasts from Cambridge write almost in their sleep." The kind of books that Orwell might have written had he been to Cambridge and belonged to the literary set, like Cyril Connolly, instead of taking the lonely course of the outsider.

Nevertheless, though his books earned him no money to speak of – he calculated he earned an average of £3 a week in the Thirties by his pen, including reviewing – he did get some encouraging notices from top reviewers. The star author of the moment, J. B. Priestley, whose *Angel Pavement* had been loftily squashed by "Eric Blair" in *The Adelphi* as mere "holiday reading", called *Down and Out* "uncommonly good reading and a social document of some value." By 1934, when it had been followed by *Burmese Days* and *A Clergyman's Daughter*, Compton Mackenzie pronounced: "No realistic writer during the last five years has produced three volumes which can compare in directness, vigour, courage and vitality."

In 1935, Orwell's bleak view of life and dour struggle for recognition was softened by the best piece of fortune he ever had – meeting Eileen O'Shaughnessy, who was to become his wife. They met at a party. He apparently told someone present even then that he was going to marry her. Later that year he wrote – "She is the nicest person I have met for a long time. However, at present, alas! I can't afford a ring, except perhaps a Woolworth's one." Characteristically he pointed out his ineligibility, when he

Eileen O'Shaughnessy, Orwell's first wife. They were married in 1936. Eileen died unexpectedly in 1945 while having an operation.

"practically proposed", within weeks of their meeting. In June, 1936, they married. "It is very rash, of course, but we talked it over and decided I should never be economically justified in marrying, so I might as well be unjustified now as later . . . I don't see myself ever writing a best-seller."

The wedding was at the small village of Wallington, near Baldock in Hertfordshire, where Orwell had taken a primitive 300-year-old cottage which had been the village stores. He re-opened the shop, on a scale so modest as to be almost pointless, taking nineteen shillings the first week and thirty shillings the next. The minute profit in due course just about paid the rent of seven shillings and sixpence, and Orwell threw himself into raising vegetables and keeping chickens. "We found we could rub along remarkably with spuds," he wrote later. There was a lightening of his natural gloom at this time: not only had he found the woman he wanted to marry, he had escaped from London, which he detested, into the sort of natural country life he had always sought. And he had been paid a £500 advance, a large sum, by Victor Gollancz to investigate the lives of people in the depressed areas of the North of England and produce a book about them.

Eileen O'Shaughnessy had many of the qualifications for the exacting role of wife to George Orwell. The daughter of a customs official, with a degree in English from Oxford, she had been in turn a teacher, a secretary, and was now studying educational psychology at London University. She was nearly thirty, with dark brown, wavy hair, large round blue eyes, a milky white complexion, and a look of innocence that belied her sophisticated intelligence. Her first task was to throw herself into the village sweetshop trade, selling children sweets by the ha'porth (four sweets) or the penn'orth (seven), while Orwell sat writing upstairs or dug his garden, which included a patch on the other side of the road where he later kept goats.

At their wedding reception, held in a local pub, Orwell's mother and sister told Eileen they were sorry for her because of the task she was taking on, but she seems to have had no other ambition than to help him fulfil himself. "She was not a dumb, adoring wife. Her logical mind improved his style, which had a certain crudity and calculated exaggeration," wrote her friend, Elisaveta Fen; and Lettice Cooper, another friend, gave as her opinion: "She shared his political views but less solemnly." Having been warned that they would have to live like the working class, without electricity, bathroom or indoor lavatory, Eileen was amused to be told by her husband on their honeymoon that they must get a proper marmalade dish: it would not do to serve it straight from the pot.

Shortly before they married, Orwell went North, in January and February of 1936, to investigate working class life in Wigan, Liverpool, Sheffield, and Barnsley for the book that was to be called *The Road to Wigan Pier*. For the first time he was confronting the real working class, the miners of the Lancashire and Yorkshire coal fields, and reporting the biggest social issue of the day, mass unemployment, from the inside. He was "living the news", as Fleet Street would put it. But he found it much harder to be accepted by the working class than by the tramps, who lived below the class boundaries altogether. Wisely he made no attempt to disguise his status as an outside investigator. He lived in miners' houses, washed in their kitchen sinks, and as an "honorary proletarian", drank in their pubs: "but though I was among them and I hope and trust they did not find me a nuisance, I was not one of them and they knew it even better than I." Indeed he complained in his diary of these two months, "I cannot get the men to treat me precisely as an equal. They call me either 'Sir' or 'Comrade'." Of the two, he disliked Comrade more – "a ridiculous label which, even after long practice, can hardly be

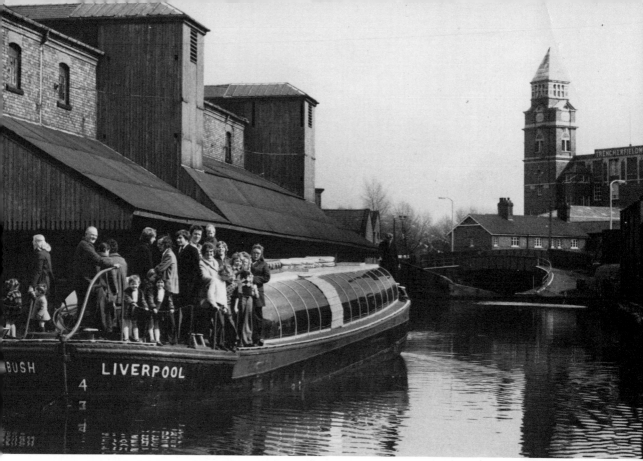

Wigan Pier. The original pier was used for loading coal onto canal barges. It later became the subject of a music-hall joke. The projecting wooden jetty had already gone when Orwell visited Wigan.

Orwell's first lodgings in Wigan, at 72 Warrington Lane. Shortly afterwards he moved into "digs" above a tripe shop.

mentioned without a gulp of shame."

Wigan Pier is an uneven and disparate collection of essays. Its early documentary passages are as powerful as any Orwell wrote on Burma, or the Paris and London underworld. The tripe shop-cum-lodging house where he stayed in Wigan is unforgettable, with its invalid landlady, Mrs Brocker, on the kitchen sofa, littering the floor with crumpled balls of newspaper on which she had wiped her mouth. "On the day there was a full chamber-pot under the breakfast table, I decided to leave." Equally lurid are the pictures of life at the coal face, the miners' noble bodies "like hammered iron statues", the inferno they work in "like my mental picture of hell", and the discovery that "the work would kill me in a few weeks". Travelling bent double underground, Orwell found his exhaustion so great that he could hardly stumble along, while the miners *ran*, on all fours, like dogs. And he reports one of those "moments" of recognition, as he did in Burma, when in a Wigan back alley he sees a young woman poking a stick up a blocked leaden waste pipe. At that moment she looked up and caught his eye "and her expression was as desolate as I have ever seen." In that moment, Orwell believes they shared the same feelings. "She understood as well as I did how dreadful a destiny it was to be kneeling there in the bitter cold, poking a stick up a foul drainpipe." He used her as an image of the sheer hopelessness of the Depression.

Orwell calculated that there were not merely two million unemployed at that period but six million sharing the dole and up to ten million underfed people depending on less than a living wage or hand-out. But it is in the diary he kept that one senses Orwell's own shock, not merely at the conditions but at the ugliness of industrial Britain. His journey is punctuated by such notes as: "frightful place" . . . "about the most dreadful places I have seen" . . . "one of the most appalling places I have ever seen". Wigan Pier itself, long demolished, once stood on a muddy canal amid "a frightful landscape of slag heaps and belching chimneys", where Orwell found rats "running slowly through the snow, presumably weak from hunger." He used it for his title because it was a grim North Country joke – if you couldn't afford to go to Blackpool, you would say you would take your holiday on Wigan Pier.

Orwell did not really see the most typical section of the English working class at close quarters. The tripe shop lodgings were far from typical. But he found, as he had found in Burma, a caste system in operation, of rulers and ruled, of exploiters and exploited – and he himself was unalterably a member of the ruling caste, just as he had been unalterably white. The second part of *Wigan Pier* is a wrestling bout with the concept of class, and what is to be done to remove it, in which Orwell's chief antagonist often seems to be himself.

Those who have claimed that Orwell resigned from his own class and tried to join the working class have misunderstood the nature of his struggle. He was far too acutely conscious of the potency of English class consciousness to believe that any such barrier jumping was possible. His attitude to the working class was two-sided, like his attitude to the natives. In *Wigan Pier* occurs his well-known picture of a working-class interior on a winter evening after tea: "When the fire glows in the open range, when Father, in shirt-sleeves, sits in the rocking chair at one side of the fire reading the racing finals, and Mother sits on the other with her sewing, and the children are happy with a penn'orth of mint humbugs and the dog lolls roasting himself on the rag mat." It might be an oil painting hung at the Royal Academy in Victorian days under some such title as "Poor But Contented" or "Honest Toil's Reward".

But it was certainly not in Wigan that Orwell saw and longed to be part of such an interior, if indeed it was anywhere outside his own imagination (he says it is a memory of what he sometimes saw in his pre-war childhood). The interiors he shared in Wigan, he repeatedly tells us, smelt. And that brings him to the four frightful words which caused more offence than any other passage in the book: "The lower classes smell. That was what we were taught – *the lower classes smell* . . . In my childhood we were brought up to believe that they were dirty, that there was something subtly repulsive about a working-class body; you would not get nearer to it than you could help . . . you thought of those layers of greasy rags and, under all, the unwashed body, brown all over (that was how I used to imagine it) with its strong, bacon-like reek." And Orwell goes on, reckless of whom he is offending, to say candidly that is just how he did feel. The most dreadful thing he could imagine as a child was to drink out of a bottle after a navvy. The smell of the company of British soldiers he marched with in Burma turned his stomach, although he liked them. "All I knew was that it was *lower class* sweat that I was smelling and the thought of it made me sick." It is difficult to see how Orwell was ever supposed to have tried to join a class lower than his own: his nose would never permit him.

On the basis of this deepest of prejudices, smell, Orwell builds a theory of class which makes socialism all but impossible for a middle-class person to embrace, much as he wanted to embrace it. He accurately places himself as a member of "the lower-upper-middle class", or the landless gentry, whose income was hardly higher that that of the better-paid section of the working class but who considered them as "common", with coarse faces, hideous accents and gross manners. Orwell maintains that a middle class person professing socialism still drinks his soup silently and will not eat cheese with his

This warehouse converted into a makeshift dwelling accurately reflects the poverty of the '30s in the average Northern industrial town.

knife – nor, he might have added, spoon the marmalade straight from the pot. And at the first real contact – a fight with a drunken fish porter on a Saturday night, for instance – he will plunge back into the snobbish prejudices of his class. This leads him into his comic catalogue of Left-wing cranks and humbugs, which caused anguish and torment to Victor Gollancz and the members of his Left Book Club for whom it was intended. "Socialism", says Orwell, "calls up a picture of vegetarians with wilting beards, of Bolshevik commissars (half gangsters, half gramophone), of earnest ladies in sandals, shock-headed Marxists chewing polysyllables, escaped Quakers, birth control fanatics, and Labour party backstairs crawlers." Contrasting this crankishness with his own elementary concept of Socialism as "justice and liberty" and the overthrow of tyranny, he snorts: "If only the sandals and the pistachio-coloured shirts could be put in a pile and burnt, and every vegetarian, teetotaller and creeping Jesus sent home to Welwyn Garden City to do his yoga exercises quietly!"

Repelled by this unappetising collection, the middle classes, he feared, would embrace Fascism. He does not seem to have considered that there might be other middle class Socialists, besides himself, who were *not* cranks. Even if there were, the chasm of class was likely to prove unbridgeable because it permeates one's whole character. "To abolish class distinctions means abolishing part of yourself. It is not enough to clap a proletarian on the back and tell him he is as good a man as you are."

Orwell later modified this still-Edwardian view of exaggerated English class-divisions to take account of the wartime extension of the middle-class both upwards and downwards, and the fading away of the collarless, unshaven (and probably malodorous) pre-war proletarian. In the end he ceased to believe they smelt. What he was right about was the durability of snobbery and class-distinctions in some form or other. "We all rail against them but very few people actually want to abolish them." They still flourish forty years later when nearly everybody claims to be middle class. But at the time, his home truths caused enormous offence. The wonder is that Victor Gollancz published the book unaltered, even with a long disclaimer as a preface ("I know of no other book in which a member of the middle class exposes with such complete frankness the shameful way in which he was brought up to think of his fellow men," he wrote apologetically. "He is a frightful snob still, and a genuine hater of every form of snobbery.")

But the book, like the year he wrote it, 1936, marked Orwell's conversion from being a patchy, uneasy novelist of the dingy Thirties into a political and polemical writer. His ideas of Socialism were still hazy and undefined, but he wrote, "Every line of serious work I have written since 1936 has been written *against* totalitarianism and *for* democratic socialism as I understand it . . . Looking back I see that it is invariably where I lacked a *political* purpose that I wrote lifeless books and was betrayed into purple passages, decorative adjectives and humbug generally."

And as the Left Book Club members opened this unpleasant surprise he had given them in the club's limp orange covers, Orwell was already in Spain experiencing the nearest thing he would ever find to a classless society.

Chapter Four
Spain

"I have had a bloody life a good deal of the time but in some ways an interesting one," wrote Orwell to an Old Etonian friend in mid-1936. He did not know it, but his life was about to become far bloodier and more interesting, thanks to the Spanish Civil War. It produced his best piece of sustained reporting, both of a war and of a revolution. Anyone who wants to know what it feels like to be in either has only to read *Homage to Catalonia*.

When the Fascist forces, led by General Franco, rebelled against the Republican government of Spain on July 18, 1936, people of Left-wing sympathies everywhere felt passionately committed to the Republican cause. At that time the involvement of the Communists in the Spanish government and the arms it was soon getting from Stalinist Russia only confirmed to many the rightness of the cause. At last, it seemed to Orwell, democracy was standing up to Fascism. Two thousand volunteers from Britain went out to fight Franco in the International Brigade, in the spirit of crusaders for a new world, a dream of socialist brotherhood come true. They were a mixture of workers and intelligentsia, doctrinaire Communists and poets. Poets like Auden and Spender volunteered for service of a propagandist kind, others like Julian Bell and John Cornford died in the fighting. Among the exalted wave of idealists, as soon as he had delivered the manuscript of *Wigan Pier* in December, went Orwell.

He went out with ideas of writing articles as a war correspondent, leaving his bride of six months to cope with the shop, the garden and the chickens. At the last moment he and Eileen pawned the Blair family silver to make sure that he should have enough money with him (she explained its absence to his mother by saying she had sent it away to have the family crest engraved on it). He travelled through France on a train packed with German, French and Czech volunteers which the peasants in the fields of southern France greeted with the anti-Fascist salute. After a glimpse of the volunteer troops in Spain, Orwell said that, by comparison, he was a trained soldier and he decided to join one of the militias. He took with him a letter of introduction from the Independent Labour Party in Britain, addressed to their representative, John McNair, in Barcelona. He told McNair that he intended not only to write a book but "to do a spot of fighting" and chose to join not the International Brigade, nor the Communist nor the Anarchist militias but the small, dissident Marxist group known as the POUM – the *Partido Obrero de Unificacion Marxista* or Workers' Party for Marxist Unity, which was hated by both the Stalinists and Trotskyists. He was given a fortnight's training at the Lenin barracks and sent to the Aragon front.

Spain immediately provided two experiences which affected him profoundly. First, he arrived in Barcelona at a moment when, as he put it, the working class was in the saddle and class distinctions seemed to have broken down. "Waiters and shop-walkers looked you in the face and treated you as an equal. Everyone called everyone else *Comrade* and *Thou*. Tipping was forbidden. All private motor cars had been commandeered . . . Practically everyone wore rough working class clothes, or blue overalls . . . In outward appearance, the wealthy had practically ceased to exist." He did not understand it all, "in some ways I did not even like it, but I recognized it immediately as a state of affairs worth fighting for." In that atmosphere, joining the militia "seemed the only conceivable thing to do." And, on joining, he saw immediately at the Lenin barracks an unknown Italian volunteer in a shabby uniform, with a fierce, pathetic,

Three fellow-travellers: W. H. Auden, Christopher Isherwood, and Stephen Spender. Orwell displayed contempt for what he considered to be their naive and misguided infatuation with Soviet Communism.

Orwell (holding cigarette) at the Aragon Front, 1937.

innocent face who asked his nationality and then grasped his hand "as if bridging the gulf of language and tradition in utter intimacy."

Orwell never saw the Italian militiaman again but he never forgot him. Like shooting the elephant, it was one of his moments of insight. When the war was over he remembered the Italian and the moment of identification they shared: two complete strangers brought together in a foreign land by a common ideal to be fought for. Recalling him six years later in the essay *Looking Back on the Spanish War*, Orwell wrote: "I see clearly that there was at any rate no doubt as to who was in the right. The central issue of the war was the attempt of people like this to win the decent life which they know to be their birthright." And, in his honour, he printed the tenderest poem he ever wrote, the only one indeed which is not ultimately a message of disillusion. It ends:

> The thing that I saw in your face
> No power can disinherit,
> No bomb that ever burst
> Shatters the crystal spirit.

Orwell was soon made a corporal in charge of twelve men in that inexperienced army with outdated weapons, such as the 1896 German Mauser rifle with a corroded barrel which he was at first given. But he found in the militias raised by the trade unions and Left

(above) *A mealbreak during the siege of Huesca, 1937. Orwell is second from the right.*
(below) *Orwell and Eileen near Huesca, March 1937. Orwell is the tall figure in the centre of the picture.*

wing parties something he had dreamed of among the slag heaps of Wigan – social equality. "Everyone from general to private drew the same pay, ate the same food, wore the same clothes and mingled on terms of complete equality . . . when you gave an order you gave it as comrade to comrade. There was a nearer approach to perfect equality than I had ever seen." He also admits he was appalled by the lack of discipline. You could only get orders obeyed by force of personality and he says he made himself "thoroughly unpopular".

Although his first taste of war was one of cold, lack of sleep, boredom and discomfort – he was disgusted to find that the two front lines were out of one another's rifle range so they shouted insults at each other – his descriptions of being at the front are oddly exhilarating. Not that he wasn't frightened or bored. His first 115 days in the line seemed one of the most futile of his life from the outer world's point of view, but they taught him a comradeship he could not have learned any other way. "One was among the tens of thousands of people, mainly of working class origin, all living at the same level and mingling on terms of equality. In theory it was perfect equality and in practice it was not far from it. There is a sense in which it was true to say that one was experiencing a foretaste of Socialism. Many of the normal motives of civilized life – selfishness, money-grubbing, fear of the boss – had simply ceased to exist."

It could not last; Orwell was ready to admit that. But in the militias he had found true democracy and glimpsed the nearest thing on earth to a classless society, which is what he believed true Socialism would bring. And, he adds with curious emphasis, "After all, *instead of disillusioning me*, it deeply attracted me." It was that discovery he must have been referring to when he wrote to Cyril Connolly from Spain: "I have seen wonderful things and at last really believe in Socialism, which I never did before." This vision was something that became part of him from then onwards. "No one who was in Spain during the months when people still believed in the revolution will ever forget that strange and moving experience. It has left something behind that no dictatorship, not even Franco's, will be able to efface."

But in the immediate present he was to see not wonderful, but deeply disillusioning things. Eileen had arrived out in Spain in February to work as secretary to John McNair and had visited her husband at the front. Now, on his first leave, they were together in Barcelona to witness the riots which were the first crack-up in the alliance of the Leftist parties fighting Franco. Orwell was politically naive when it began. He hardly distinguished between the Stalinist, Marxist, Trotskyist and Anarchist parties, with their confusing sets of initials. He saw them all simply as brother anti-Fascists like himself and, if asked what he was fighting for, would have answered equally naively, "Common decency." Now he learned fast that common decency was not a virtue much practised between rival factions of the Left.

The POUM, like the Anarchists, were working for actual revolution and in Catalonia, the province centred on Barcelona, the revolution had already taken over to a considerable degree. Workers had seized factories, peasants had taken over land from the rich landowners, churches had been closed and looted and workers had organized their own militias. There was a struggle between those who thought the revolution should continue, and those who thought it should not be allowed to interfere with the war with Franco. Then Orwell discovered that the Communist Party was working not to postpone the revolution but to make sure it never happened. This was on the orders of Moscow. The Soviet Union had no intention of undermining its alliance with France by

Orwell at the Independent Labour Party Summer School at Letchworth, in Hertfordshire, 1937. John McNair, who was with the Orwells in Barcelona, is on the far left.

encouraging a workers' revolution just south of the French border. Since Moscow was supplying the Republicans with arms, its demands were obeyed.

The Communists, and the right-wing Socialists in the Republican government, ruthlessly suppressed the revolutionaries on their own side. It branded them as "Trotskyists" and traitors, "disguised Fascists", secretly in league with Franco. The paradoxical situation was reached where the chief anti-revolutionary force was the right-wing Communist Party, defending capitalism. When Orwell got back to Barcelona, the classless appearance of the crowds in the streets was gone. The bourgeois had come back out of hiding. "Fat prosperous men, elegant women and sleek cars were everywhere."

It was on May 3 that the Civil Guards, acting for the Government, seized the telephone exchange, which was operated by the Anarchists. The gunfire heard from the building was the signal for the explosion that everyone had felt was bound to come between the rival powers. Barricades went up in the streets and flags of the competing parties flew from the buildings they occupied.

Orwell was issued with a rifle at POUM headquarters in a hotel on the Ramblas and was posted in an observatory on the roof of a cinema opposite, with orders not to fire unless attacked. Hungry and bored, he spent three days and nights up there, reading a succession of Penguin books from England, when he was not "marvelling at the folly of it all." The city of a million people was locked in "a nightmare of noise without movement . . . Nothing was happening except the streaming of bullets from barricades and sandbagged windows. The trams stood motionless where their drivers had jumped out of them when the fighting started. And all the while the devilish noise went on, like a tropical rainstorm . . . what the devil was happening, who was fighting whom and who was winning was at first very difficult to discover."

Later, Orwell came to the conclusion that the fighting was unplanned and caused by the workers coming on to the streets spontaneously rather than by their party leaders ordering them to do so. "So far as one could judge from what people were saying at the time there was no real revolutionary intention anywhere." But when the fighting spontaneously died away five days after it started the blame for the "insurrection" was fixed upon the POUM, only 70,000 strong, "the weakest party and the most suitable scapegoat."

One of the results of the Barcelona fighting was the breaking up of the separate militias, which were distributed among the units of the Popular Army. The other was a steady propaganda campaign against the POUM in the Communist press, leading to its total suppression and the imprisonment or stealthy execution of its leaders the following month as "Franco's Fifth Column". Thanks to his affiliation with this group, Orwell learned what it was to be the victim of political persecution. He saw, behind the propaganda of anti-Fascism, the ruthlessness of equally totalitarian Stalinism.

Before this happened he went back to the front as a junior officer with the British I.L.P. contingent. He was hit on May 20 by a bullet which passed straight through his throat from front to back, just missing the spine and carotid artery but paralysing one vocal chord and leaving him temporarily speechless. Orwell observed his own reactions as if he were an interested outsider – "no pain, only a violent shock, such as you get from an electric terminal: with it a feeling of utter weakness, of being stricken and shrivelled up to nothing . . . I had a vague feeling of satisfaction. This ought to please my wife, I thought. She always wanted me to be wounded, which would save me from being killed when the great battle came." Typically he understated it in his letters: "My wound was not much but it ought to have killed me, in fact for a few minutes I thought it had, which was an interesting experience." He also admitted to feeling "a violent resentment at having to leave this world which, when all is said and done, suits me so well. The stupid mischance infuriated me. The meaningless of it!" He was not, as has sometimes been suggested, a man with a death-wish.

His baptism as the target of political terrorism, which awaited him on his return from hospital to Barcelona, was theatrical. As he walked into the hotel lounge where his wife was sitting, she got up, put an arm round his neck and, smiling sweetly for the benefit of the onlookers, hissed in his ear: "Get out! Get out of here *at once*!" As she led him downstairs, protesting, a French friend added: "Get out quickly and hide yourself before they telephone the police!"

When they were outside in the street, Eileen revealed to him that the POUM had been declared illegal in his absence, its offices closed, its headquarters seized, everyone connected with it put in prison, including all forty members of the Executive. Andres Nin, the POUM leader, had been arrested in his office, put in prison in Madrid and was

The POUM militia at the Lenin Barracks, Barcelona, January 1937. Orwell is at the very rear of the column.

never heard of again. Most of their friends had been arrested. Two nights earlier six plain-clothes police had burst into their room at the hotel and searched it, taking away every piece of paper, including Orwell's diaries and letters, but not their passports and chequebooks. These were hidden under the mattress and the Spanish police could not bring themselves to order a woman to get out of bed. What also luckily escaped detection were his notes for *Homage to Catalonia*. He had been sending them back from the front written on whatever he could find, backs of envelopes, even toilet paper. Eileen typed them out in McNair's office in Barcelona. When police ransacked McNair's flat, he hid the manuscript on the window ledge. When he was caught with some of it in his bag he argued his way past the police by saying it was written by "a friend of Harry Pollitt" – secretary of the British Communist Party – "to rouse the English comrades from their lethargy."

The question now was how they could get away without being arrested too. If Eileen disappeared, the police would immediately search for them. So she remained at the hotel while Orwell, exasperated, protesting his innocence and badly in need of a good night's sleep, was persuaded by his wife that he must sleep out, in hiding. "Patiently she explained the state of affairs. I was guilty of 'Trotskyism.' The fact that I had served in the POUM militia was quite enough to get me into prison. It was no use hanging on to the English notion that you are safe so long as you keep the law." So, tearing up his prized POUM militiaman's card, he went off sulkily to find a roofless church to sleep in – "I had so wanted a night in bed."

At night Orwell was a fugitive criminal, but by day, mingling with the crowds, he and Eileen could live an almost normal life by passing themselves off as English tourists. "We went to expensive restaurants and were very English with the waiters." Orwell relieved his feelings after they had eaten by writing POUM slogans on the walls in large letters. But he soaked up, for future reference, the nightmare atmosphere of constantly changing rumours, censored newspapers and ubiquitous armed men . . . something unknown to political writers in England. In England, he wrote, the notion of liquidating everyone who happens to disagree with you does not yet seem natural. "It seemed only too natural in Barcelona . . . It was as though some huge, evil intelligence were brooding over the town." He knew the double life of the hunted man under totalitarianism. The Stalinists were in control of Barcelona, but the effect for Orwell would have been no different if it had been Franco and the Fascists.

After five days on the run, they had managed to get their passports stamped. "Those five days were the most exciting of my life," wrote McNair. "Orwell was solid all through the time – thought only of his wife and his book." Together they crossed the frontier into France in the dining car of a train, looking respectable enough not to be questioned by the detectives on board. Orwell reflected grimly that entering Spain six months before he had been advised to take off his collar and tie; now the one salvation was to look bourgeois.

Once out of the nightmare, the Orwells immediately wished they were back again. They stayed a few days near the frontier recuperating by the sea, and found the relief from the tension of Spain was a bore and a disappointment. "Both of us wished we had stayed to be imprisoned along with the others." Conscious of how ineffectual his part in the war had been, Orwell returned to England to pay his "homage" to his comrades in the form of a book. The last page of it describes the incredible contrast between the harshness of warring Spain and the sleekness of peaceful Southern England, seen from the boat train – the deep meadows, the posters telling of cricket matches and royal weddings, the red buses, the blue policemen – "all sleeping the deep, deep sleep of England, from which I sometimes fear that we shall never wake till we are jerked out of it by the roar of bombs."

Now it was his task to try to wake up the English, to disperse the fog of lying propaganda which combined with native complacency to produce a state of ignorant apathy about Spain. He was conscious of the fact that he was one of the very few outside observers who knew what had really happened in Barcelona. His friends had been betrayed, arrested, imprisoned without trial, some of them shot. All were falsely labelled as traitors and saboteurs in league with Franco and the Fascists. He owed it to them to clear them of the charge and to expose the cynicism of the Stalinists who fabricated it.

And when he tried to do so he found almost no one would let him speak. As soon as he got into France, he cabled the *New Statesman* offering them an article on his experiences, to which they said yes. When they saw the article was about the suppression of the POUM they said they couldn't print it because it would "cause trouble". They then sent him a book to review, *The Spanish Cockpit*, but refused to print his scathing exposure of Communist tactics in reviewing it. This "controverted the political policy of the paper", in the words of its editor, Kingsley Martin. (Orwell published a similar review of the book in *Time and Tide* and an exposure of the lies put out by the Communists in the *New English Weekly*, but neither were papers of much influence compared with the *New Statesman*.) Next, his publisher, Victor Gollancz, said he would not be able to publish

Orwell's book. Though not a word of it was yet written, he heard that Orwell had been associated with the POUM and knew the inside story of the Barcelona riots. That was enough.

It should be said that Orwell was not such an enthusiastic supporter of the POUM as he appears in his book. He did not accept their belief that they could win the war by pressing ahead with the revolution. "I always told them they were wrong and refused to join the party," he wrote to a fellow-combatant soon after arriving back in England. He admitted that he made his book more sympathetic to them than he actually felt because they had been libelled as traitors and Fascists in the Communist-inspired press.

He never forgave Kingsley Martin for refusing his articles exposing this injustice. After an interval of two years he resumed his contributions to the *New Statesman*. But when lunching with Malcolm Muggeridge at a restaurant on one occasion he asked him to change places so that Muggeridge, and not himself, would be facing Kingsley Martin at a neighbouring table.

It was not surprising that Orwell became slightly paranoid about what he saw as "pro-Communist censorship" in England. "It is impossible to get a word about all this mentioned in the English press," he wrote in one letter – "all this" meaning the wholesale jailings and beatings of his friends accused of being "Trotskyists". The Communist command of the Press, he wrote in another, extended to the whole of the Capitalist anti-Fascist press including such papers as the *News Chronicle*, because they realized that official Communism was now anti-revolutionary. "The accounts of the Barcelona riots beat everything I have ever seen for lying." He added that he himself was being denounced in the *Daily Worker* as a Fascist, Trotskyist, etcetera. "It was almost impossible to get any publicity in the English press for a truthful account of what was happening in Catalonia. The huge 'Trotsky–Fascist' plot which the Communist press claimed to have discovered was given wide publicity. The fact that members of the Government denied that there was any truth whatever in the 'plot' story was carefully unmentioned . . . No denial was published except in very obscure papers and, half-heartedly, in the *Daily Herald* and *Manchester Guardian*."

Looking back later he wrote: "This kind of thing is frightening to me because it gives me the feeling that the very concept of objective truth is fading out of the world. Lies will pass into history." *Nineteen Eighty-Four* began for him there and then.

Orwell himself said that the Spanish War taught him where he stood as a committed, political writer. Fredric Warburg offered to publish his book on Spain through his new, independent Left-wing publishing house, Secker and Warburg. He offered an advance, large for those days and for a struggling publisher, of £150. This was timely. According to McNair of the I.L.P., Orwell was very hard up and "the party instructed me to do what I could to alleviate matters. He would never accept money, only a few meals." Orwell told McNair of his political feelings. "He had quite definitely decided to have nothing more to do with Victor Gollancz or the Communist Party or any of their fellow-travellers. He would not join the I.L.P. All political parties were 'self-seekers'. He never hated the Communist Party. He simply had the deadly, public-school scorn for them. He told me that they were not worth hating."

Back at the Stores in Wallington, Orwell was watching the inevitable victory of the Fascists, with their superior weapons, draw nearer in Spain. "It is heartbreaking to see the way things have gone," he wrote to Cyril Connolly, "Nearly a million men dead in all, they say, and obviously it is going to be all for nothing . . . I am writing against time to

Victor Gollancz, Orwell's first publisher. He wrote a disclaiming preface to **The Road to Wigan Pier,**
and refused to publish **Homage to Catalonia** *even before it was written.*

come out in March. I have already had to change my publisher."

He finished *Homage to Catalonia* in January, 1938, and it was published in April while the war was still in the balance. Despite its brilliant reporting and important political analysis, "it caused barely a ripple on the political pond", in the words of Fredric Warburg. Of 1500 copies printed, 683 were sold in the first six months, and thereafter only a trickle. When Orwell died in 1950, there were still copies of the first edition lying unsold in the warehouse. Orwell had not even earned the £150 advance on his royalties.

Obviously he had to find some other way of "turning political writing into an art." "My starting point is always a feeling of partisanship, a sense of injustice," he confessed in *Why I Write*. His books were written primarily to expose some lie, to get attention for some overlooked fact. "My initial concern is to get a hearing." But he added, even in such a frankly political book as *Homage to Catalonia*, "I did try very hard to tell the whole truth without violating my literary instincts." The results, for all his literary skill, were complex reading and his unpopular opinions were widely ignored. Even now, it is one of his least-read books. It was because of this devastating disappointment that he began to search for, and brood on, a political allegory that everyone could understand.

Fredric Warburg, who published **Homage to Catalonia** *and later* **Animal Farm** *after three publishers had turned it down.*

Chapter Five
His Country Right or Left

As Europe moved towards the war with Hitler that Orwell had felt to be inevitable since 1936, he himself entered a period of frustration, confusion and near despair. *Homage to Catalonia* was unsympathetically reviewed and sank without trace – except to make him *persona non grata* with English Left-wingers. By the time it appeared, in April 1938, Orwell was in a Kent sanatorium with his first attack of tuberculosis to be diagnosed (he had probably suffered earlier, undiagnosed attacks). For six months he was a helpless patient, forbidden to write, and in September, on doctors' advice that he should spend winter in a warm climate, he and his wife went to Morocco for six months.

The Spanish War and his illness meant that his earnings were very meagre: only the vegetables and chickens he raised at Wallington, a pound or two of income from the shop and a little book reviewing. The novelist, L. H. Myers, sent Orwell £300 anonymously through a friend to enable him to winter abroad. Orwell accepted it as a loan (as soon as he received any royalties on *Animal Farm*, he paid it back) and he and Eileen went to stay in Marrakech. The fruit of this six-month stay was his novel *Coming Up For Air*.

Coming Up For Air was the last book of conventional fiction he ever wrote and in many ways the most depressing, for its theme is that of an England already ruined by its own folly and about to be smashed to pieces by bombs. Yet in spite of the horrors of industrialism and mass marketing already brought about by "the stream-lined men", and the vision of the destruction to come from the skies, the images that remain in the mind afterwards are those that Orwell conjures up of life in rural England before 1914. Although for once he chose a narrator who was in every way his own opposite – George Bowling, insurance salesman, fat, forty-five, with false teeth and a bowler hat – he calls up an idyllic picture of the England of his own boyhood.

George Bowling's "Lower Binfield", a market town near the Thames in Oxfordshire, is a kind of amalgam of Henley and Shiplake where Orwell spent his boyhood and school holidays. Despite the deliberately unliterary style – the book is written as if Bowling were telling the story in a pub – the atmosphere is entrancingly captured of sleepy, hot afternoons in an eternal summertime of horses and horse-

Henley-on-Thames, where the Blair family settled on their return from India. Orwell's childhood memories of the place contributed to his portrait of Lower Binfield in **Coming Up For Air**.

Orwell never lost his boyhood love of fishing and expressed it through the character of George Bowling in **Coming Up For Air**.

troughs, of old-fashioned sweets called Farthing Everlastings and the dust and smells of the traditional seedsman's shop. There are pages saturated in sunlit nostalgia like a child's picture book, which perhaps Orwell only felt able to indulge in under the vulgar disguise of George Bowling, to avoid the accusation of sentimentality.

It must be very closely based on his own memories. Its outstanding quality is the happiness of his remembered passion for fishing. Fishing for the coarse fish of the ponds, river and secret pools of Lower Binfield is described in loving detail as an almost sacred activity, a guarantee that those who indulge in it are decent and trustworthy, and knew a peace of mind that has since vanished. "The very idea of sitting all day under a willow tree beside a quiet pool belongs to the time before the war, before the radio, before aeroplanes, before Hitler . . . Where are the English coarse fish now? When I was a kid every pond and stream had fish in it. Now all the ponds are drained, and when the streams aren't poisoned with chemicals from factories they're full of rusty tins and motorbike tyres."

George Bowling longs to get away from his nagging wife, children and life in the suburbs in order to rediscover the peace of his childhood world at Lower Binfield and, especially, to fish a secret pool full of giant carp, which he only glimpsed as a boy. When he finds it, it is, of course, drained and full of tins. Everything has changed, except the graveyard. The town, swollen and industrialized, is making bombs. His father's seedsman's shop has turned into a fake-antique "Wendy's Teashop". His pilgrimage tells him that the old life is finished and to go looking for it is a waste of time. "There's no way back to Lower Binfield."

The loss is not merely that of a more peaceful, comely and rural England but of a sense of stability. "People then had something we haven't got now. They didn't think of the future as something to be terrified of . . . they didn't feel the ground they stood on shifting under their feet." They believed thrift, hard work and fair dealing would see them through bad times as well as good – and that the English order of life would not let them down by changing. "For ever and ever, decent God-fearing women would cook Yorkshire pudding and apple dumplings on coal ranges, wear woollen underclothes and sleep on feathers, make plum jam in July and pickles in October and read *Hilda's Home Companion* in the afternoons with the flies buzzing round in a cosy little underworld of stewed tea, bad legs and happy endings."

It is essentially the same vision as Orwell gave of ideal working class domesticity in *The Road to Wigan Pier*. It is in many ways sentimental, for it leaves out poverty, anxiety, sickness and dirt. Bowling conjures up a kind of bovine idyll for people who do not want to think. Orwell himself could not have stuck it for five minutes.

Coming Up For Air was Orwell's most determined attempt to write an imaginative novel from the viewpoint of a character other than himself. He failed in this, comparatively speaking, though it was his most successful novel to date. Years later he wrote to Julian Symons: "You are perfectly right about my own character intruding on the narrator. I am not a real novelist anyway and that particular vice is inherent in writing a novel in the first person." *Not a real novelist anyway.* There – it was out. He had faced it. The best he could do in that line, to use his own phrase, was "Wells watered down". George Bowling was a Mr Polly who found there was nowhere to escape to. Orwell's problem was that the orthodox novel form did not suit him. "One has masses of experience that one passionately wants to write about, e.g. fishing, and no way of using them up except by disguising them as a novel." He had not yet discovered how to use them as an essayist or journalistic columnist.

The book marked the beginnings of a change in Orwell's emotional outlook that the war would soon intensify. George Bowling loved the past too much ever to be a revolutionary. Orwell *was* a revolutionary and yet he looked back on rural life before the First World War almost as idyllically as Bowling. He thought he had no allegiances. Not to the traditions of the ruling class, with which he had so dramatically broken. Not to the revolutionary theorists of the Left, after the betrayals he had seen in Spain. But now he discovered an allegiance to a traditional England that went to the roots of his own deeply English character. This conflict of emotional loyalties was to form his strange succession of attitudes to the approaching war, which changed his political stance even more than the Spanish war had done.

Orwell began by opposing the war as an imperialist manoeuvre. In 1937 he wrote to Geoffrey Gorer (one of the few reviewers who had appreciated the importance of *Homage to Catalonia*): "Everyone with any imagination can foresee that Fascism, not of course called Fascism, will be imposed on us as soon as the war starts . . . If one collaborates with a capitalist-imperialist government against Fascism, i.e. a rival imperialism, one is simply letting Fascism in by the back door." This was the beginning of an obstinately wrong-headed phase in Orwell's thinking which lasted well into the war itself. He was led astray by applying what he thought were the lessons of Spain to England, without allowing for the great differences that national character produces. He took a crudely Trotskyist attitude that one imperialism is just as bad as another, including the British variety, and briefly espoused a sort of pacifism.

In June, 1938, he joined the Independent Labour Party (under whose auspices he had gone to Spain) and gave, for its journal, his reasons: "I believe the I.L.P. is the only party which is likely to take the right line either against imperialist war or against Fascism, when this appears in its British form." In September he wrote from Morocco, "If war does break out, I don't think I shall come home . . . The whole thing seems to me so utterly meaningless that I think I shall just concentrate on keeping alive." In early 1939 he was writing to Herbert Read that it was vital "for those of us who oppose the coming war" to start organizing for "illegal, anti-war activities" while it was still possible to buy a printing press and stocks of paper for producing underground pamphlets. "I doubt whether there is much hope of saving England from fascism of one kind or another but clearly one must put up a fight."

Yet by the end of that year he was complaining that he could not get war work or join up. "It seems to me that now we are in this bloody war we have got to win it and I would like to lend a hand." What changed his outlook, he tells us, was a dream he had on the night before the Stalin–Hitler pact was announced in August, 1939. He dreamed that the war had already started. And although he had always looked forward to it as a dreaded nightmare, the thing he felt in his dream was simple relief. His dream revealed to him that "I was patriotic at heart, would not sabotage or act against my own side, would support the war, would fight in it if possible. I came downstairs to find the newspaper announcing Ribbentrop's flight to Moscow. So war was coming and the Government, even the Chamberlain Government, was assured of my loyalty." (*My Country Right or Left.*)

At a stroke, both his bogeymen, Hitler and Stalin, had lined up on the same side and it cleared his mind wonderfully, blowing away his disgusted pacifism like fog. He left the I.L.P. and tried hard, though unsuccessfully, to get into the fighting. It was a bitter disappointment for him to be rejected repeatedly for any kind of military service because of his chest. His wretched health, he said, had never prevented him from doing anything he wanted to do – "except fight in the present war." "It is all very well to be 'advanced' and 'enlightened', to snigger at Colonel Blimp," he wrote, reviewing Malcolm Muggeridge's book, *The Thirties*, "but a time comes when the sand of the desert is sodden red and what have I done for thee, England, my England?" In this ironic reference to the jingoist verse of Sir Henry Newbolt and W. E. Henley, he was staking out a new position as a revolutionary patriot. Pessimist as he was, he refused to believe with Muggeridge that the game was up for England. Some great disaster, he felt, would settle the matter one way or the other. Dunkirk and the fall of France were only a month away when he wrote the words.

Meanwhile, Eileen had joined the Censorship Department in Whitehall and had gone to live at her brother's house in Greenwich during the week – he had been called up to serve as a surgeon with the R.A.M.C. and she kept her sister-in-law, Gwen, company. Orwell stayed at Wallington with the chickens, the ducks, Muriel the goat, and his dog Marx, growing potatoes against the famine he confidently expected but feeling impotent creatively. The sales of *Coming Up For Air* had been killed by the outbreak of war and he found he could not write fiction in wartime conditions. Instead he turned to essay-

Orwell feeding Muriel the goat at Wallington, summer 1939.

writing and thereby discovered the gift for which he is perhaps most admired today – the gift of clear-sighted and ruthless literary-political analysis teamed with a hard-edged clarity of expression. It was a new development, for his previous autobiographical descriptive pieces such as *Shooting an Elephant* are not essays but documentary sketches. He began with the longest essay he ever wrote, the wonderful *Charles Dickens*.

It is a genial labour of love – there are passages in it to make any Dickens-lover exclaim aloud with pleasure at Orwell's perception of his characters – and yet it is a severe, as well as penetrating assessment. Dickens is not allowed to get away with anything. His manifest shortcomings as a radical, his ignorance about and aloofness from the working class, his contempt for political solutions, his horror of revolution and of the mob, the raw proletariat of his day, his disinterest in what people did for a living, are all laid bare under Orwell's searching gaze. So is Dickens' inadequate idea of a "happy ending", a huge, prosperous family doing absolutely nothing but "constantly multiplying like a bed of oysters" and enjoying a sort of "radiant idleness". And yet Orwell hails Dickens as the subversive writer he clearly was, a man deeply concerned about the way power is abused by the haves over the have-nots, the strong over the weak, the elders over the young, the oppressors over the oppressed. Dickens, he declared, "as a matter of course is on the side of the underdog, always and everywhere", and not for the first time in the essay, one feels he is speaking not just for Dickens but for himself.

The same applies to the passages about Dickens' "decency", a quality not much remarked by previous literary commentators. Both men were moralists at heart and to express memorably "the native decency of the common man" was Dickens' supreme achievement in Orwell's eyes. When, on the final page, he visualized Dickens' face, not the historical face of the photographs but the face the writer of such books *ought* to have, he seems to be telling us a great deal about the image he would like to have seen in his own mirror: "He is laughing, with a touch of anger in his laughter, but no triumph, no malignity. It is the face of a man who is always fighting against something, but who fights in the open and is not frightened, the face of a man who is *generously* angry." Orwell, too, was always fighting against something but up to this point his laughter had been overborne by his anger and his anger had been more often resentful than generous. That

In a memorable essay, Orwell contrasted the Victorian gentleman crook Raffles with the contemporary "shocker" **No Orchids for Miss Blandish**.

The American writer Henry Miller, whom Orwell met in Paris in 1936, en route to Spain. Miller told him that to go to Spain at that time was "the act of an idiot."

Richard Rees' oil painting of "Orwell's Bedroom" – a study of Van Gogh-like simplicity.

A scene from the stage version of **No Orchids for Miss Blandish**. *Orwell strongly disapproved of its cruelty and sadism – and its success.*

was gradually to change as, in 1940, he entered upon the most fruitful decade of his life – and the last.

Inside the Whale, the title essay of the collection when it was published in March of that year, is a curious mixture of the relevant and the dated. It is most interesting when it analyses why the Auden-Spender-MacNeice-Day Lewis movement of literary intellectuals had turned to Communist Russia as their mythical promised land – unlike Orwell. He is rather simplistic in suggesting that it was a bloc transfer of old, unfashionable loyalties: that the new substitutes for patriotism and religion were Russia and Stalin, respectively. Orwell gets in his shrewdest blow when he says that the soft life of the English middle class intelligentsia allows them to swallow totalitarianism, complete with purges, imprisonment without trial, summary execution and the rest because they have no idea what such horrors are like. Auden's line in his poem *Spain* – "The conscious acceptance of guilt in the necessary murder" – (a line he later altered) is singled out. It could only be written "by a person to whom murder is at most a *word*. Personally I would not speak so lightly of murder. I have seen the bodies of numbers of murdered men."

Orwell had just apologized for his "spiteful" description of Auden some years before as "a sort of gutless Kipling", but what he was now saying was just as damaging. Here was the Spanish War veteran with wounds to show for it hitting at those who had gone out there primarily as voyeurs (Auden had a vague job as a propagandist well behind the lines). Here was the Old Etonian who had earned his stripes as a proletarian among the kitchen slaves of the Latin Quarter, the tramps of the Spike and the unemployed miners of Wigan sneering at the public school Left-wingers who had, in many cases, served their time as public school masters. Above all, he was pillorying pre-war Left-wing orthodoxy. While Auden and his generation were boasting of their faith in Stalinist Russia, he had been denouncing it. "Why should *writers* be attracted by a form of

Socialism that makes mental honesty impossible?" he demanded sarcastically.

These reflections are strung from what is ostensibly an appreciation of the early novels of Henry Miller, the writer who remained apolitical, passive, irresponsible, cushioned from reality "inside the whale" like a modern Jonah. These passages read curiously now, for Orwell seems to attach far more significance to Miller's work than it will bear. Orwell enthused over *Tropic of Cancer*, partly, perhaps, because it was the sort of novel he may have wanted to write about the Paris of the 1920s which both he and Miller experienced. But his praise of Miller as "the only imaginative prose writer of the slightest value who has appeared among the English-speaking races for some years past" seems ludicrously extravagant, even if he *is* being used as a stick to beat Auden and Spender. Only two years later he was admitting that Miller's later work, beginning with *Tropic of Capricorn,* was "poor stuff". Miller thought Orwell "a foolish idealist".

The other essay written at this time, *Boys' Weeklies*, was the first of his sociological-literary pieces on what would later be called Pop Art. These include *Good Bad Books, Raffles and Miss Blandish, The Art of Donald McGill* and the *Decline of the English Murder*. No one before him had found such subjects worth notice. *Boys' Weeklies* half affectionately castigates the *Magnet* and the *Gem*, and their successors, for being stuck in the dream world and naive mentality of 1910. Ironically, Orwell's recent novel had just pointed out how much more enjoyable life in England *was* in 1910 when, as he put it in the essay, the King was on his throne and the pound was worth a pound. Unexpectedly, the essay produced a witty reply from Frank Richards, the prolific author of the Greyfriars stories in the *Magnet* and the St Jim's stories in the *Gem* for over thirty years. He claimed that human nature, especially among boys, is dateless. He was unrepentant about the absence of social conscience, Left-wing views or sex from his stories, or the fact that he made foreigners out to be funny – "I must shock Mr Orwell by telling him that foreigners *are* funny." He added that boys' minds ought not to be disturbed and worried by politics and, unlike Orwell, he hoped that a boys' paper with a Left-wing bias was impossible and would remain impossible. In that hope he seems to have been well justified.

It is curious to reflect that the inventor of Billy Bunter, of all the people who duelled with Orwell in print, is the one who came off best and, to many minds, outpointed him. Orwell emerged from the encounter looking a bit too solemn, a bit like the Owl of the Remove, especially in his suggestion that the tone of the *Magnet* and the *Gem*, etcetera, was deliberately intended by their proprietors to maintain the class structure. "A study of these noblemen's more important papers," wrote Evelyn Waugh some years later with tongue in cheek, "reveals a reckless disregard of any such obligation . . . Mr Orwell betrays the unreasoned animosity of a class-war in which he has not achieved neutrality." *Touché*.

During the retreat of the B.E.F from France and in the expectation that the bombing would soon start, Orwell closed up his cottage at Wallington and moved to London where he and Eileen occupied a succession of flats near Regents Park, in St John's Wood and Maida Vale. They were relying on her income as a civil servant. He had no job in prospect other than freelance reviewing. He reviewed theatre and films for *Time and Tide*, books for Cyril Connolly's *Horizon* – which also published *Boys' Weeklies* and many subsequent essays by Orwell – and wrote more book reviews for *Tribune*, to which he soon began to add articles.

He also began a wartime diary, which he maintained sporadically for two years. In it,

WONDERFUL COMPLETE SCHOOL STORY and FREE PHOTO-PLATE
INSIDE.

The MAGNET 2ᴰ

"KEEP YOUR MOULDY PLUMS!" HOOTED BUNTER.

No. 1,323. Vol. XLIII.   EVERY SATURDAY.   Week Ending June 24th, 1933.

...k Richards, creator of Billy Bunter and prolific author of school stories in the **Magnet** *and the* **Gem**.
...'s famous reply to the essay **Boys' Weeklies**, *he surprisingly turned the tables on Orwell.*

on June 10, when the Germans were poised to take Paris, he wrote: "Everything is disintegrating. It makes me writhe to be writing book reviews at such a time." At this time he was visiting London stations where troops and refugees were arriving from France, to seek news of Eileen's brother, Laurence. There was no news: he had been killed on the beaches at Dunkirk.

Orwell was still hoping to "fake my way past the doctors" and join up. He failed. Instead he joined the Home Guard in St John's Wood, immediately its formation was announced. With previous fighting experience in Spain to his credit he was made a sergeant in charge of a section of twenty men. Among them he soon recruited his publisher, Fredric Warburg, who became his corporal. Orwell had to find his own forage cap, since caps larger than size 7 were a great rarity, and Warburg recalled in his book *All Authors Are Equal* that he wore it perched so jauntily on the side of his head that he feared it would fall off. "I discerned the zeal which inflamed his tall, skinny body. His expression was Cromwellian in its intensity." Warburg pointed out that the Home Guard had many of the qualities Orwell valued in a fighting force – it was unprofessional, voluntary, anti-Fascist, rather inefficient and animated by a deep affection for England.

Over a quarter of a million men volunteered in the 24 hours following the first broadcast appeal, and they were soon followed by a million more. Orwell was reminded of the militias which volunteered to defend the Spanish republic. Somewhat naively he supposed that the same revolutionary spirit might be roused in them as well. In December, 1940, he was writing in *Tribune* to urge its Left-wing readership not to regard the Home Guard as a "Fascist organization" but to join it in sufficient numbers to turn it into a People's Army. "Without a radical change in our social system the war cannot be won . . . A million men with rifles in their hands are always important . . . the existence of a popular militia, armed and politically conscious will be of profound importance." In short, the Home Guard was a heaven-sent opportunity to get rifles into the hands of the workers and the Socialists.

Of course, the Home Guard never became a politically conscious force either of the Left or the Right. To Orwell's disgust it was mainly officered by middle-class retired Army officers, many of whom were having the time of their lives in once more having soldiers to play with. He told Warburg once that if the invasion occurred, he expected them to defect to Hitler. Warburg disagreed. "You never know, Fred," he said darkly.

Orwell was a fervent believer in guerrilla training and attended the Osterley Park training school run by Spanish War veterans under Tom Wintringham. Men like them were fiercely impatient of the elderly Blimps in the senior ranks. "The usual senile imbecile," he noted of one inspecting general – "the men, however, very ready to be inspired." What sort of account they would have given of themselves will never be known and the Home Guard is now chiefly remembered as "Dad's Army" for its comic possibilities. In any case it ceased to matter, as the threat of invasion steadily receded, and Orwell resigned on health grounds in 1943. When he came to look back on it, he realized that what had held the force together had nothing to do with his own revolutionary fervour: it was inspired by a primitive instinct to defend one's home ground. But the fact that over a million men could be given rifles to keep at home without the least threat to public order impressed him as an indication of the stability of British democracy.

The first satisfying outlet he was offered for his patriotic energies was an invitation to

A march-past of the Home Guard in North London. Orwell joined up as a sergeant in 1940.

write the first of a series of two-shilling pamphlets called *Searchlight Books*. They were published by Warburg and edited by Orwell and Tosco Fyvel, a Jewish expatriate with guerrilla experience in pre-war Palestine, who was later to succeed Orwell on *Tribune*. *Searchlight Books* claimed to offer constructive ideas for Britain's post-war future. Orwell's text was entitled *The Lion and the Unicorn* and subtitled "Socialism and the English genius". The first part of it was to become better known when republished separately as *England Your England*.

Written during the Battle of Britain and the Blitz, when the invasion looked only too imminent, it spurred Orwell to examine both his reasons for loving England and the features of the English social system that he hated. In doing so he re-wrote the text of English patriotism, which had hitherto remained stuck in the grooves of Victorian and Edwardian empire-conscious vainglory. Schoolboys were still reared on the complacencies of *Our Island Story*. Orwell's list of his country's virtues was far less conventional. He emphasized its gentleness. Among English peculiarities he instanced with approval were the dislike of the military, policemen without revolvers, good-tempered bus conductors and "the old maids biking to Holy Communion through the mists of the autumn morning." English culture, to Orwell, is bound up with solid breakfasts and gloomy Sundays, suet puddings and red pillar boxes. However much you hated it or laughed at it, he reminded his readers, "you will never be happy away from it for any length of time." He spoke like an exile returned, which in a sense he was at that

moment. "The crowds in the big towns, with their mild knobby faces, their bad teeth and gentle manners, are different from a European crowd." The words "mild" and "gentle" sing out of that sentence.

Orwell's catalogue of English characteristics included the privateness of English Life, the addiction to individualistic hobbies. "We are a nation of flower-lovers but also a nation of stamp-collectors, pigeon fanciers, amateur carpenters, coupon snippers, darts players, crossword puzzle fans . . . All the culture that is most truly native centres round the pub, the football match, the back garden, the fireside and the 'nice cup of tea'." This pleasure in private, mostly solitary pursuits appealed to Orwell as a keen, but inexpert, carpenter, smallholder and naturalist, who noted down in the midst of wartime London a heron overflying Baker Street or a kestrel killing a sparrow in the middle of Lord's cricket ground. He approved the English delight in bawdiness, belief in the incorruptibility of British justice, deeply moral attitude to life and their emotional unity which enables them to feel and act together in moments of supreme crisis. But he soon comes to what he considers the chief English vice: "England is the most class-ridden country under the sun. It is a land of snobbery and privilege, ruled largely by the old and silly . . . It resembles a family, a rather stuffy Victorian family in which the young are generally thwarted and most of the power is in the hands of irresponsible uncles and bedridden aunts . . . A family with the wrong members in control."

The rest of *The Lion and the Unicorn* is devoted to the decay of the English ruling class, Orwell's *bête noire*, which he condemned as effete, stupid, unteachable and a danger to the nation because of its "infallible instinct for doing the wrong thing." With such people in charge, he doubted whether the war could be won. He still believed an "English Revolution" was imminent and he went on to try to imagine the sort of England that might emerge if class privilege were abolished by an English form of socialism. He saw a country whose major resources were nationalized, where incomes were scaled down so that the highest did not exceed the lowest, after tax, by more than ten to one, and where there was a single classless education system. He saw most of these aims at least partly accomplished by the post-war Labour Government and the Butler education act – but he was wrong in thinking they could be accomplished by popular pressure in the middle of a war of survival. With the enemy at the gate, the instinct of his fellow-countrymen was to stick to what they knew.

Orwell was right in seeing that the war was the greatest forcing agent of social change there had been in his lifetime. But he over-estimated its pace. When P. G. Wodehouse was led away by the Germans, he wrote: "The whole of that way of life is being destroyed too completely to survive even in fantasy. Blandings Castle is full of evacuees. Bertie Wooster's shares have slumped to nothing. Baxter is in the Ministry of Information. A bomb has demolished the Drones Club." And in *My Country Right or Left* he visualized the revolution transforming England within two years, maybe a year. "I dare say the London gutters will have to run with blood. All right, let them, if it is necessary." And he proceeded, in a deliberately provocative pamphleteering phrase, to prophesy "Red militias billeted in the Ritz."

In fact, David Niven, Peter Ustinov and the Army Kinematographic Service were to be billeted in the Ritz, dreaming up encouraging war films. P. G. Wodehouse would live to revisit Blandings Castle – and to be defended by Orwell for staying in his fantasy world. The English Revolution was going to be gradual, partial and, in accordance with his own favourite national characteristic, far more *gentle* than he imagined.

The London Blitz. "You can't leave when people are being bombed to hell." The Orwells stayed and were bombed out of their flat in Maida Vale.

P. G. Wodehouse. Orwell was the first to defend him in print after the creator of Jeeves had been accused of collaborating with the Nazis.

Orwell's mistake was wishful thinking and an excessive obsession with class. Even his admiration for Churchill was grudging because he was a member of the ruling class. "Is it not a frightful commentary on the English socialist movement that at this date, the moment of disaster, the people still look to a Conservative to lead them?" he demanded querulously in an essay on *Fascism and Democracy* in 1941. He returned to the subject of class in an essay called *The English People* written in 1944 and later published as a pictorial book. By then, he admitted, exaggerated class distinctions were being ironed out by the war. "The tendency of the working and middle class is evidently to merge. Another ten years of all-round rationing, utility clothes, high income tax and compulsory national service may finish the process once and for all." There were almost another ten years of such privations but they didn't finish the process.

In the same year, 1944, Orwell admitted how wrong he had been about the English Revolution in one of the wartime London Letters he contributed regularly to the New York *avant-garde* literary magazine, *Partisan Review*. He had been grossly wrong in his analysis of the political mood until the end of 1942, he declared candidly. "I fell into the trap of assuming that 'the war and the revolution are inseparable'." After quoting many more of his misjudgments, he asked: "How could I write such things?" His answer illustrates his inclination to hot-headed generalization followed by a likeable readiness to admit he was wrong. "I don't share the average English intellectual's hatred of his own country ... I hate to see England either humiliated or humiliating anybody else. I wanted to think we would not be defeated and I wanted to think that the class distinctions and imperialist exploitation of which I am ashamed would not return ... I exaggerated the social changes that were actually occurring and underrated the enormous strength of the forces of reaction."

But though he had misjudged the temper of the English people fighting a war of survival, Orwell was not far wrong about their desire for change after the war. And in recognizing how his wishful thinking had led him astray, he resolved to learn the lesson: "I believe that it is possible to be more objective than most of us are, but that it involves a *moral* effort." From then onwards he tried to rise above his subjective feelings and make allowances for them. Meanwhile, if he had not actually invented Left-wing patriotism, he had made it intellectually respectable.

An unusally relaxed and benign Orwell with an animal friend at the home of Mabel Fierz, in Hampstead.

Chapter Six
The Road to Animal Farm

The one front line that Orwell was allowed to be in was the London Blitz. He came up to London specially for it and stayed throughout the war. When telling Julian Symons how much he hated living in the capital, he continued: "But you can't leave when people are being bombed to hell." Going to sleep to the sound of gunfire reminded him of Spain, where he found the sound a soporific. Watching the fires raging beyond St. Pauls from Cyril Connolly's rooftop, he was struck by "the size and beauty of the flames" but not by the historical significance of the occasion – unlike Connolly who said, rather portentously, "It's the end of capitalism – it's a judgement on us." Ever alert to the uses of language, he noted in his diary the advent of the word "blitz" to mean any kind of attack, whether lightning or not. "'Blitz' is not yet used as a verb, a development I am expecting." Three weeks later, like a collector of the wild flowers of common speech, he noted: "The *Daily Express* has used 'blitz' as a verb."

Eileen, who had shared the perils of Barcelona with enjoyment, was just as steadfast now. She was on the telephone to him when a bomb fell in Greenwich Park opposite her brother's house. There was a pause in the conversation and a tinkling sound. "What's that?" he asked. "Only the windows falling in," she replied. She left censorship and in April, 1942, joined the Ministry of Food in Portman Square where her job was to organize the early morning broadcasts of recipes, called the "Kitchen Front". She shared an office with the novelist, Lettice Cooper, who remembered her vividly: "Small with blue eyes and nearly black hair; pretty, with very pretty hands and feet and a body beautifully poised on her legs. She generally walked as if she wasn't thinking where she was going. Often I used to meet her in the lunch-hour, drifting along Baker Street deep in thought . . . She and George were always hard up, bombed out and in difficulties, but always helping somebody else and never really ruffled."

Eileen told Lettice Cooper how she had been coming down the staircase of their block of flats when a bomb dropped nearby. A terrified elderly woman resident was crouching down in the hall. "Eileen saw George kneeling by her with his hand on her head, patting her and 'looking like Christ'. Both he and Eileen were among the most fearless people I met." They were also generous with their rations. Eileen brought her a pound of sugar for the all-night vigils at her warden's post and said George's reaction was to ask why she wasn't giving them *all* their sugar.

The death of her brother Laurence at Dunkirk was a very heavy blow. Eileen once said that if she were in trouble, he would have come from the other side of the world, but that George would not, because for him work always came before anybody – a judgement others have confirmed. Orwell does not seem to have noticed how Eileen's always delicate health was deteriorating in wartime conditions, or if he did, he was unable to take special care of her, working as always at full stretch and devoting all his spare time to Home Guard duties and fire-watching.

On top of his reviewing and pamphlet-writing, in August, 1941, he took a job with the BBC's Eastern Service and was put in charge of talks broadcast to India. He described the BBC atmosphere as "something halfway between a girls' school and a lunatic asylum." The department was housed in the entire ground floor of an Oxford Street department store, divided by inadequate partitions and full of clatter. Orwell was fiercely convinced that India (and Burma) should be independent as soon as possible.

Orwell in his role as talks producer for the BBC Eastern Service, broadcasting to India. T. S. Eliot is seated in front of Orwell and fellow producer, William Empson, is standing on the right.

Part of his task was to convince his Indian speakers, most of them anti-British intellectuals, that by aiding the British war effort they would hasten the end of the British Raj, which was by no means self-evident. Orwell was acutely aware that so few English-speaking Indians possessed short-wave radios that his propaganda war was practically useless.

What irritated him above all about the BBC was the feeling of frustration engendered by bureaucratic changes of course. "One is constantly putting sheer rubbish on the air because of having talks which sound too intelligent cancelled at the last moment . . . Even when one manages to get something fairly good on the air, one is weighed down by the knowledge that hardly anybody is listening." The over-staffing also oppressed him . . . "Hundreds of skilled workers, costing the country tens of thousands per annum, and tagging on to them are thousands of others who have found themselves a quiet niche and are sitting in it, pretending to work."

Nevertheless, he often got "something fairly good" on the air, fielding an impressive team of speakers such as E. M. Forster (on Gibbon), T. S. Eliot (reading his own poetry), Dylan Thomas, Stephen Spender, Edmund Blunden, Herbert Read and many friends, such as Connolly. The programmes were highbrow, a sort of university extension course for Indian students, which seems an odd indulgence in a desperate war situation. Thanks to Orwell they were on a higher intellectual level than anything the Home Service was providing at the time.

One of his own literary contributions was an imaginary interview with his hero, Jonathan Swift. He told his listeners that when he opened his eighteenth-century Collected Edition, which he had bought at a farmhouse auction for five shillings, he could *hear* Swift speaking to him and see his three-cornered hat, snuff-box and spectacles. *Gulliver's Travels*, he said, had meant more to him than any other book ever written. Since he first read it at about eight years old, he doubted if a single year had passed without his rereading part of it and yet – he told the imaginary Swift – "I can't help feeling that you laid it on a bit thick." Swift, said Orwell, had been too hard on humanity. He had not believed human nature could change and therefore he could not see that life was worth living. Human beings, even if dirty and ridiculous, Orwell told the great Dean, were "mostly decent". Bertrand Russell summed up this difference between them in an aphorism: "Orwell hated the enemies of those whom he loved, whereas Swift could only love (and that faintly) the enemies of those whom he hated."

Orwell's propaganda duties were to deliver a weekly news commentary, which he broadcast in a flat and monotonous voice. "I was often with him in the studio and it was painful to hear such good material wasted," recalled one of his colleagues, John Morris. The BBC, with its multifarious departments, memos and canteen, where the wartime stew was no doubt thin, may well have served as Orwell's model for the Ministry of Truth in *Nineteen Eighty-Four*. The seeds of "Hate Week" may have lain within the Eastern Service's propaganda line against the Japanese, but he seems to have regarded the work he did there as fairly truthful even by his high standards of truth. "I consider I have kept our propaganda slightly less disgusting than it might otherwise have been," he wrote, though he also described himself, near the end of his service, as "an orange that has been trodden on by a very dirty boot." After two "wasted" years, he sent in his letter of resignation, saying he would be more usefully employed in journalism. John Arlott, who inherited his desk, remembers him as an aloof, gaunt figure in a tightly belted raincoat: "He was fed up with the BBC – but he would have been fed up with any kind of regimentation."

Within a week of leaving, he had become literary editor of *Tribune*. He was already contributing occasionally to *Tribune*, and to *Horizon* and the *New Statesman*, and had begun to write articles and book reviews for the *Observer* at the invitation of its future editor, David Astor. One of his earliest contributions was on the need to grant independence to India – "He always liked to test what a paper would permit him to say," said Astor. The *Observer* passed the test and he continued to write for it until the year before he died. But it was *Tribune*, "the one paper in England," he wrote, "which had neither supported the Government uncritically, nor opposed the war, nor swallowed the Russian myth", which got the best of Orwell, the journalist. It was then directed and edited by Aneurin Bevan, the charismatic conscience of the Labour Party and future Minister of Health, whose fiery personality gave the paper its tone. The two men never became close but Bevan gave Orwell the freedom to write as he pleased.

"As I Please" was the title under which his column appeared weekly from December, 1943, until February, 1945, on the paper's centre-spread – on the borderline between the political front half and the literary and arts section, Orwell's ideal territory. The column won a considerable following and it is still readable, in large measure, nearly forty years later because it reflects such an idiosyncratic and generous

AS I PLEASE : by George Orwell

weeks ago, in the course of some on schools of journalism, I carefully scribed the magazine the *Writer* as defunct." As a result I have a severe letter from its proprietors, close a copy of the November issue *Writer* and call on me to withdraw ment.

draw it readily. The *Writer* is still d seems to be much the same as ough it has changed its format since it. And I think this specimen copy examining for the light it throws ls of journalism and the whole business extracting fees from struggling free-urnalists.

rticles ate of the usual type (" Plot-chnique (fifteenth instalment,") by A. Bagley, etc.), but I am more d in the advertisements, which take e than a quarter of the space. The of them are from people who pro-be able to teach you how to make out of writing. A surprising undertake to supply you with ready-ots. Here are a few specimens.

tting without tears. Learn my way mplest method ever. Money returned atisfied. 5/- post free.

xhaustible plotting method for women's 5 3d. Gives real mastery. Ten days' ial."

OTS. Our plots are set out in sequence dy for write-up, with lengths for each ce. No remoulding necessary just quisite clothing of words. All types ed."

OTS: in vivid scenes. With striking g lines for actual use in story. Speci-onversation, including authentic dialect. rt-short, 5-. Short story, 6 6d. Long-ete (with tense, breathless 'curtains')

8 6d. Radio plays, 10 6d. Serial, novel, novelette (chapter by chapter, appropriate prefix, prose or poetical quotations if desired). 15 6d. -1 gn."

There are many others. Somebody called Mr. Martin Walter claims to have reduced story-construction to an exact science and " eventually evolved the Plot Formula according to which his own stories and those of his students throughout the world are constructed. . . . Whether you aspire to write the ' literary ' story or the popular story, or to produce stories for any existing market, remember that Mr. Walter's Formula *alone* tells you just what a ' plot ' is and how to produce one." The Formula only costs you a guinea, it appears. Then there are the " Fleet Street journalists " who are prepared to revise your manuscripts for you at 2 6 per thousand words. Nor are the poets forgotten:

"GREETINGS.

"Are you poets neglecting the great post war demand for sentiments '?

Do you specialise and do you know what is needed ?

Aida Reuben's famous Greeting Card Course is available to approved students willing to work hard. Her book 'Sentiment and Greeting Card Publishers,' published at 3 6d, may be obtained from," etc , etc.

I do not wish to say anything offensive, but to anyone who is inclined to respond to the sort of advertisement quoted above, I offer this consideration. If these people really know how to make money out of writing, why aren't they just doing it instead of peddling their secret at 5 - a time? Apart from any other consideration, they would be raising up hordes of competitors for themselves. This number of the *Writer* contains about 30 advertisements of this stamp, and the *Writer* itself, besides giving advice in its articles, also runs its own Literary Bureau in which manuscripts are " criticised by acknowledged experts " at so much a thousand words. If each of these various teachers had even ten successful pupils a week, they would between them be letting loose on to the market some fifteen thousand successful writers per annum!

Also, isn't it rather curious that the " Fleet Street journalists," " established authors " and " well-known novelists " who either run these courses or write the testimonials for them are not named or, when named, are seldom or never people whose published work you have seen anywhere? If Bernard Shaw or J.B. Priestley offered to teach you how to make money out of writing, you might feel that there was something in it. But who would buy a bottle of hair restorer from a bald man?

If the *Writer* wants some more free publicity it shall have it, but I dare say this will do to go on with

*   *   *

ONE favourite way of falsifying history nowadays is to alter dates. Maurice Thorez, the French Communist, has just been amnestied by the French Government (he was under sentence for deserting from the army). Apropos of this, one London newspaper remarks that Thorez " will now be able to return from Moscow, where he has been living in exile for the last six years."

On the contrary, he has been in Moscow for at most five years, as the editor of this newspaper is well aware. Thorez, who for several years past has been proclaiming his anxiety to defend France against the Germans, was called up at the outbreak of war in 1939, and failed to make an appearance. Some time later he turned up in Moscow.

But why the alteration of date? In order to make it appear that Thorez deserted, if he did desert, a year *before* the war and not after the fighting had started This is merely one act in the general effort to whitewash the behaviour of the French and other Communists during the period of the Russo-German pact. I could name other similar falsifications in recent years. Sometimes you can give an event a quite different colour by switching its date only a few weeks. But it doesn't much matter so long as we all keep our eyes open and see to it that the lies do not creep out of the newspapers and into the history books

*   *   *

A CORRESPONDENT who lacks the collecting instinct has sent a copy of *Principles or Prejudices*, a sixpenny pamphlet by Kenneth Pickthorn, the Conservative M.P., with the advice (underlined in red ink) " Burn when read."

I wouldn't think of burning it. It has gone straight into my archives. But I agree that it is a disgusting piece of work, and that this whole series of pamphlets (the *Signpost Booklets*, by such authors as G. M Young, Douglas Woodruff and Captain L. D. Gammans) is a bad symptom. Mr. Pickthorn is one of the more intelligent of the younger Tory M.P.s (" younger " in political circles means under sixty), and in this pamphlet he is trying to present Toryism in a homely and democratic light while casting misleading little snacks at the Left. Look it this, for instance, for a misrepresentation of the theory of Marxism:

Not one of the persons who say that economic factors govern the world believes it about himself. If Karl Marx had been more economically than politically interested he could have done better for himself than by accepting the kindnesses of the capitalist Engels and occasionally selling articles to American newspapers."

Aimed at ignorant people, this is meant to imply that Marxism regards *individual* acquisitiveness as the motive force in history. Marx not only did not say this, he said almost the opposite of it. Much of the pamphlet is an attack on the notion of internationalism, and is backed up by such remarks as: " No British statesman should feel himself authorised to spend British blood for the promotion of something superior to British interests." Fortunately, Mr. Pickthorn writes too badly to have a very wide appeal, but some of the other pamphleteers in this series are cleverer. The Tory Party used always to be known as " the stupid party." But the publicists of this group have a fair selection of brains among them, and when Tories grow intelligent it is time to feel for your watch and count your small change.

mind. In it, Orwell developed his knack of hitting nails crisply on the head. It sharpened and hardened his style. Amid his attacks on the powerful, the dangerous and the silly, he would sprinkle his interests in simple, mundane things. He would dilate on the disproportionate pleasure given to him by some sixpenny Woolworths roses he had planted, or an out-of-the-way book he had discovered on a secondhand stall. He always had some tit-bit for lovers of useless knowledge or some new usage or misusage of the English language to remark upon or protest against.

Orwell had found the answer to the problem of how to write about the odds and ends of his experience which did not fit into fiction. His piece on the mating of toads as a symptom of the coming of Spring is a delightful combination of observation and reflection. Not everyone approved. Some readers protested at the inclusion of such frivolous, non-political material – one lady wrote indignantly that "flowers are bourgeois". More often they were offended by his comments on the Soviet betrayal of socialism. The circulation manager made a weekly estimate of the number of readers whom Orwell had offended.

Michael Foot, who succeeded Bevan as editor, maintains that Orwell was first and foremost a *Tribune* Socialist – in those days a far more middle-of-the-road form of socialism than it represents now. "No other newspaper in the land for which George was prepared to write would have printed what he wanted – and *Tribune* had several alarms, magnificently allayed by Aneurin Bevan's wisdom . . . *Tribune* sustained his pride when all Establishment doors, Right, Left and especially Centre, were slammed in his face," he wrote.

Jon Kimche, managing editor, who sub-edited Orwell's copy (and who had previously worked with him at Booklovers' Corner in Hampstead) remembers his typescripts as being exceptionally "clean". They were also delivered on time and at precisely the right length. He also remembered Orwell showing a somewhat cavalier attitude to facts and figures if they conflicted with a point he wanted to make – and being corrected at editorial conferences by the economist E. F. Schumacher, who later wrote *Small Is Beautiful.*

Orwell enjoyed writing his column far more than his task of editing the literary pages. His opinion of book reviewers and reviewing was low enough, despite the fact that he did it all his writing life. "The prolonged, indiscriminate reviewing of books is a quite exceptionally thankless, irritating and exhausting job," he wrote in *Confessions of a Book Reviewer*, "It not only involves praising trash but constantly inventing reactions towards books about which one has no spontaneous feelings whatever." The reviewer, he said, was pouring his immortal spirit down the drain "half a pint at a time".

Afterwards he told *Tribune* readers: "It is not a period I look back on with pride. The fact is I am no good at editing." He hated planning, he hated answering letters. "My memory of that time is pulling out a drawer here or a drawer there, finding it stuffed with letters and manuscripts which ought to have been dealt with weeks earlier, and hurriedly shutting it again." That, indeed, was the state of his desk according to Tosco Fyvel, when he took it over on succeeding Orwell in 1945. "I have a fatal tendency to accept manuscripts which I know very well are too bad to be printed," wrote Orwell. It showed a curious tender-heartedness in so ruthless a critic of work once it was published. As for the neglected letter-writing, one which he did write and which has been preserved is to tell a contributor that he had lost his review. "So sorry – will you do it again?"

One of *Tribune*'s virtues for him was that it only demanded his attendance three days

*Aneurin Bevan. Wartime editor of **Tribune** and later a leading member of the post-war Labour Government.*

91

A youthful Michael Foot, who succeeded Aneurin Bevan as editor of **Tribune** *in 1945. The portrait is by David Low.*

a week. There was a book in him which had been waiting for six years to get out and within the month he joined the paper, November, 1943, he began writing it.

It was when he returned from Spain in 1937 that he first began to think about *Animal Farm*. It was then that he discovered "how easily totalitarian propaganda can control the opinion of enlightened people." In England he found that the lies told by the Communists about his fellow-combatants, the POUM, had been generally accepted – just like the "confessions" of the Moscow trials during the purges had been accepted. Few people besides himself had yet realized the extent of the perversion of the Soviet revolutionary ideals of 1917 into a totalitarian society. His attempt to alert others in *Homage to Catalonia* had been, till then, a failure. So completely had the book been ignored that he might as well never have published it. Ever since, he had been searching for a way of exposing the Soviet myth which would be immediately understood by everyone. The answer occurred to him when he returned to Wallington from Spain: "I saw a little boy, perhaps ten years old, driving a huge cart-horse along a narrow path, whipping it whenever it tried to turn. It struck me that if only such animals became aware of their strength we should have no power over them, and that men exploit animals in much the same way as the rich exploit the proletariat." (Preface to the Ukrainian edition of *Animal Farm*, 1947.)

As a way of making people "see the Soviet regime for what it really was", *Animal Farm* could not be bettered. It was almost immediately hailed as a masterpiece. It was translated into thirty-nine languages. Its central slogans – "All animals are equal but some are more equal than others" and the bleating sheep's chorus of "Four legs good – two legs bad" – passed into common currency as well as into the books of quotations.

The "fit" of the allegory between the revolution on the farm and the aftermath of the Russian revolution is wonderfully apt. But it also casts the spell of a fairy story, which is what Orwell sub-titled it. It would not have done so had he not loved and understood animals – with the exception of pigs. Orwell saw no redeeming feature in any of the pigs, or Bolsheviks. Snowball–Trotsky was no better in principle than Napoleon–Stalin. He explained that Snowball had been just as guilty as the others of the first betrayal of the revolution – the commandeering by the pigs of the cows' milk which led, step by step, to greater betrayals, until the pigs were indistinguishable from the animals' old oppressors, the human beings.

"It is the history of a revolution that went wrong – and of the excellent excuses that were forthcoming at every step for each perversion of the original doctrine." So ran the original blurb, written by Orwell, and in many ways the "excellent excuses" are the most telling passages in the book. After two years of immersion in propaganda, our own and the enemy's, Orwell felt particularly keenly about its malign powers of persuasion. Squealer (a living *Pravda*) is portrayed with especial insight and loathing. His trump card is that, unless the leadership is given unqualified obedience, the old order in the shape of Farmer Jones will come back. It is the classic technique of political hoodwinking – an appeal to accept the bad in preference to the worse. Squealer is the essential tool of dictatorship. It is he who justifies the turnabouts of policy, who downgrades the reputation of the rival leader, Snowball, from hero to traitor, who doctors the original revolutionary ideals by repainting them under cover of darkness on the wall of the barn . . . and it is Squealer who is the first to be seen walking on his hind legs. He is not merely the skilled propagandist but the falsifier of history, the destroyer of objective truth. He is a one-man (or one-pig) version of the Ministry of Truth.

"A revolution that went wrong" – an allegory not merely of the Russian revolution but of all revolutions, because Orwell believed all revolutions are betrayed by the lust for power. In his essay on Arthur Koestler, written in the year in which he finished *Animal Farm*, he treated the other great work of disillusion with Soviet Communism, *Darkness at Noon*, as a masterpiece which shows that revolution is "a corrupting process". He sees in Koestler's story of the old Bolshevik who confesses to imaginary crimes, the message not merely that power corrupts but so do the violent means of attaining power. "Lenin leads to Stalin and would have come to resemble Stalin if he had happened to survive." Orwell does not quite share Koestler's resulting pessimism. "Perhaps the choice before man is always a choice of evils, perhaps even the aim of Socialism is not to make the world perfect but to make it better. All revolutions are failures but they are not all the same failure."

This was more encouragement than he was to offer in *Nineteen Eighty-Four*. And yet it is hard to find that much faith in *Animal Farm* itself. Major, the Marx–Lenin figure who inspired the revolution on Manor Farm, declared: "Our lives are miserable, laborious and short." So they remain, with even more injustice, under the animals' own régime. The wonder is that a story of such unrelenting injustice, cruelty (as in the death of Boxer, symbol of the devoted and hoodwinked proletariat) and pessimism should have appealed so strongly to people all over the world. And this in spite of the fact that never once does it betray human emotions such as pity. The style is the plainest that even Orwell achieved. The standpoint from which he narrates it is one of unconcerned objectivity, a "that's-the-way-it-is" tone of voice. The result is that it awakens a profound feeling of protest in every reader.

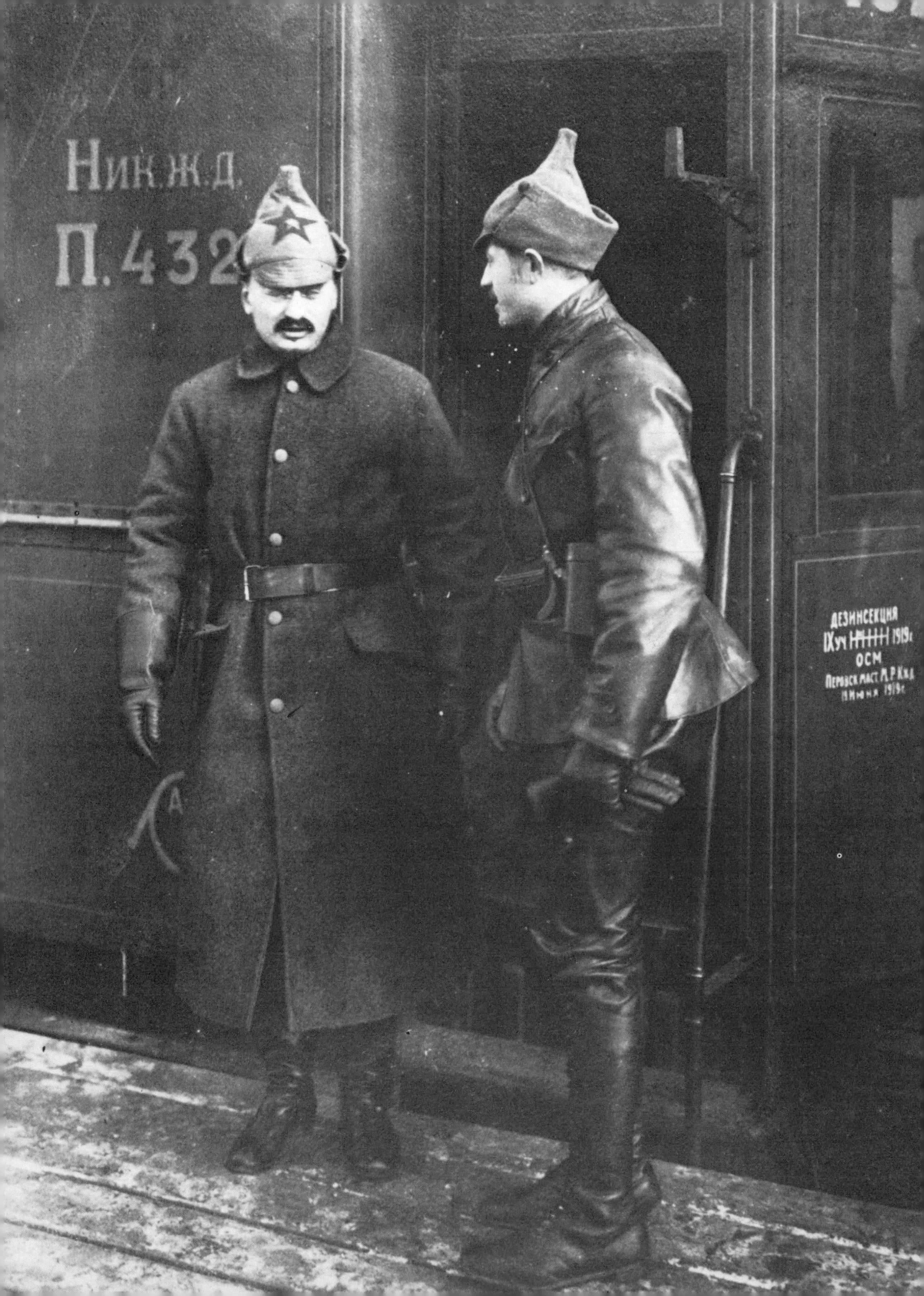
Ник.ж.д.
П.432
ДЕЗИНСЕКЦИЯ
ОСМ

Lenin and Stalin. Major and Napoleon in **Animal Farm**.

..eon Trotsky in Petrograd, 1920. Trotsky was the model for Snowball in **Animal Farm** *and for Goldstein*
in **Nineteen Eighty-Four**.

There could hardly have been a more unpopular moment to submit such a merciless exposure of Stalinism for publication. Stalin's Russia, suffering tremendous losses, seemed in early 1944 to be holding Germany at bay almost unaided, having saved Britain from any further threat of invasion. "Uncle Joe" was regarded with admiration, almost with affection in England. Orwell realized that his "fairy story" was a piece of political dynamite. "It is so not OK politically that I don't feel certain in advance that anyone will publish it," he wrote prophetically in February, as he finished it.

His uncertainty was quickly proved justified. By July, Gollancz, Jonathan Cape and Faber and Faber had all returned his manuscript. (To add to his misfortunes Orwell had been bombed out of his flat in Maida Vale.) Jonathan Cape, prompted by advice from some unknown friend of his at the Ministry of Information, suggested that the Bolsheviks should be represented by some other animal than pigs. The director of Faber's who refused it was none other than T. S. Eliot, who had also rejected *Down and Out in Paris and London* many years before. He acknowledged its merits as a fable such as "few authors have achieved since Gulliver". On the other hand he was not convinced "that this is the thing that needs saying at the moment" – in other words, it was politically inopportune. Eliot then proceeded to demonstrate that he had missed the point of the fable. The pigs, he said, as the most intelligent animals, were the best qualified to rule – "so what was needed (someone might argue) was not more communism but more public-spirited pigs." The attempt to establish equality and fair shares did not come into it: an élite was the normal and necessary condition of life to this élitist. One would like to have heard the snort with which Orwell must have read his letter.

He had now come up against an almost solid wall of self-censorship. His anguish of mind showed when he called upon his Fleet Street bookseller friend, Louis Simmons, and told him of Gollancz's refusal to publish. Simmons asked him innocently, was this quite the time to publish an anti-Russian book? According to him, Orwell exploded – "Not you, too, Simmons! I'd never have thought it of you!" – and stormed out of the shop, not to return for several months. After three rejections, Orwell was losing patience – and faith in publishers.

Fredric Warburg had asked to see it but foresaw difficulties in getting the paper allocation (under wartime rationing) to print it. "If that falls through," Orwell wrote to his agent, Leonard Moore, "I am not going to tout it round further publishers but shall publish it myself as a pamphlet at two shillings. I have already half arranged to do so and have got the necessary financial backing . . . It is important to get this book into print, this year if possible." What Orwell had done was to approach David Astor of the *Observer* to finance the printing and an anarchist poet, Paul Potts, a friend of his, who ran a small imprint called the Whitman Press which could provide a quota of paper to print it on. Neither of them had read the text or been told anything about it by Orwell. "He thought it could be done for a few hundred pounds and I said I would do it," said David Astor, "I hadn't then read the book and he wouldn't show it to me. He approached me on the basis, would I help him to say something that it was important to say? You wouldn't have asked Orwell if you could *read* it!"

At about this point Orwell wrote a special preface for the private publication, on the assumption that it would by then have been "refused by four publishers". Not surprisingly, it was a tirade against suppression and censorship, particularly the kind of self-censorship at which the English establishment is so adept because of a tacit agreement at any given time that it is "not done" to say certain things. At that time what was "not done" was to criticize the Soviet government. "Stalin is sacrosanct . . . the English intelligentsia, or a great part of it, had developed a nationalistic loyalty towards the USSR and in their hearts they felt that to cast any doubt on the wisdom of Stalin was a kind of blasphemy."

To Orwell's mind the rejection of *Animal Farm* was all part of the same process by which liberal opinion had accepted and justified the Russian purges and the lies about the Trotskyist groups fighting for the Spanish republic, and would have justified the continued banning of the *Daily Worker* or the continued imprisonment of Oswald Mosley. All these, to Orwell, were symptoms of a slide towards Fascism among our so-called liberal intellectuals and led up to his splendid summation of the real meaning of freedom of speech: "If liberty means anything at all, it means the right to tell people what they do not want to hear." He had earlier quoted Voltaire's famous statement: "I detest what you say; I will defend to the death your right to say it." He had coined a saying worthy to be put alongside it.

As it turned out, the preface was not needed because Secker and Warburg accepted *Animal Farm* for publication. But it was a near thing. According to Warburg's account, late that summer he was walking along the Strand to his office when Orwell came up to him and thrust at him a dirty typescript in a brown paper cover. "You won't like this," he said, "It's very anti-Russian. Much too anti-Russian for you." Warburg read it that evening, recognized it as a classic but also had grave doubts about the possible repercussions of publishing it. These were reinforced by his Russophile wife's passionate reaction to it. "If you publish that book," she said to Warburg, "I'll leave

First edition of **Animal Farm**, *published August 1945.*

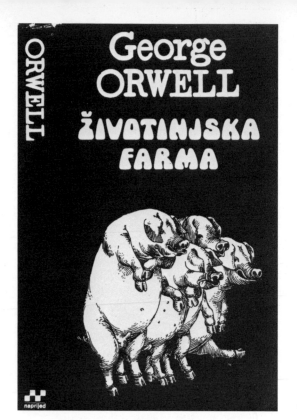

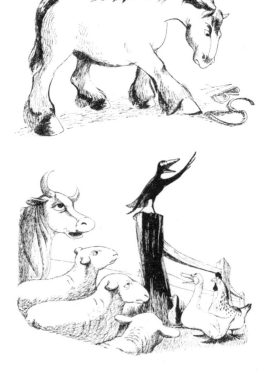

Some later editions of **Animal Farm** :
(top left) *Serbo-Croat* ; *(top right)* *Swahili!* (bottom left) *Polish* ; (bottom right) *English illustrated edition.*

you." (Pamela Warburg and Orwell, however, became close friends.) In the end Warburg agreed not with his wife but with his enthusiastic partner, Roger Senhouse, and undertook publication as soon as he could get enough paper.

In the acute shortages of the time, this took another year. In that period, the book continued to cause nervous crises. According to a letter of Orwell's, even Aneurin Bevan was afraid there would be an embarrassing row when it was published, as was then planned, just before the British General Election. American publishers turned it down with monotonous frequency – nearly twenty of them – before Harcourt Brace accepted it. One claimed it was impossible to sell animal stories in the USA.

A great deal happened in Orwell's life while he was struggling to get *Animal Farm* before the public. He at last persuaded a reluctant Eileen that they should adopt a child – she was reluctant because she doubted her capacity to love one enough and she did not want to give up her work at the Ministry of Food where she was happy. But Orwell's longing for a child had been growing more and more insistent, especially in view of the fact that he had convinced himself that he was sterile, as he told several of his

(*above*) **Animal Farm** *in Mauritian Creole.*

acquaintances. "How lucky you are to have a kid of your own!" he wrote to a friend not long before the adoption. In June, through the offices of Eileen's sister-in-law, Gwen, who was a doctor, they adopted a baby three weeks old straight from hospital, dressed him, carried him home and called him Richard Horatio Blair.

According to Lettice Cooper, Eileen became at once devoted to the child, despite her earlier misgivings, and "George was transfigured with tenderness – his great wish was that the baby should have a white perambulator with gold lines on and go to Eton." If that sounds unlikely, there is no doubt that, from the moment of Richard's arrival, Orwell put his whole being into fatherhood, getting up in the night, changing nappies and filling his letters with news of the boy's progress. Richard arrived with the Flying Bombs, or doodlebugs, one of which brought down the ceilings of their flat in Maida Vale. A friend lent them a flat off Baker Street until they found a new home, the top floor of 27, Canonbury Square, in a then shabby and unfashionable part of Islington. It meant a lot of stairs up which to manoeuvre a baby or a pram.

They were not destined to share their new home for long. In February, 1945, Orwell gave up the literary editorship of *Tribune* because he had been invited by David Astor to go to liberated Paris, and thence into Germany, as a war correspondent for the *Observer*. Leaving Eileen to cope with the baby, he went to Paris in March, 1945, and stayed, like all allied war correspondents, at the Hotel Scribe near the Opéra. There he found "among the huge tribe of American journalists with their glittering uniforms and stupendous salaries, not one had heard of *Tribune*" – but the French correspondents had, for his columns had often been translated and extracts published in *Libertés*. "Ah, vous êtes George Orwell!" exclaimed a large man in black corduroy breeches and crushed his hand with a handshake. Among the stupendously-salaried Americans at the Scribe was Ernest Hemingway, who produced a bottle of Scotch from under the bed when Orwell introduced himself. He, at least, knew the name.

According to Astor, Orwell's real object was to get to Germany as soon as possible in order to breathe the air of a totalitarian state before events had changed it. He travelled on to Cologne in March, was taken ill with lung trouble and hospitalized at the end of March – ill enough to draw up notes for his literary executor. He there received a telegram telling him that his wife was dead. She had died under the anaesthetic before an operation. She had gone up to Newcastle with Richard to stay with her sister-in-law's children and their nurse. She had been feeling ill for some time, far more seriously than Orwell appears to have realized. No doubt she kept it from him. She had been to a doctor who diagnosed a growth and what Orwell later told his friends was to be a minor operation, was in fact to have been a hysterectomy. He discharged himself from hospital, having filled himself up with tablets, and returned to England. It was the worst moment of the most traumatic year of his life.

The most tensely awaited moment of that year came just over a week after the atom bombs on Hiroshima and Nagasaki were exploded in August. Thin and drab as it looked in its wartime economy binding and cover, *Animal Farm*, too, was the literary equivalent of an atom bomb. Its first printing, of only 4,500 copies, was sold out within two weeks. Apart from a stony silence in Communist papers, the reviews were glowing and Orwell, after all his struggles to get it published, was surprised by its "friendly reception". He must have known it was more than just a very good book. He may have guessed it was his immortality. But characteristically, he found something left to be desired. "Not one of the swine," he complained to a friend, "said it was a beautiful book."

Orwell with his adopted son Richard, shortly after the death of his wife, Eileen.

Chapter Seven
Nineteen Eighty-Four

The death of his wife was a subject that Orwell found too painful to talk about. Except to a few intimates, his references to it were so bare and laconic that they sound unfeeling. "My wife died last week, she was going to have a minor operation and died while she was having it," he told Julian Symons, and went on immediately to talk about conditions in occupied and defeated Germany. One attempt at expressing sympathy, from John Morris of the BBC, brought the reply, "Yes, it is most inconvenient. I don't know how I shall be able to look after the child." Within a week he had settled Richard with a "sort of aunt" and had gone back to Paris. From there he went on to Germany to take his mind off what had happened. There was no break in his weekly despatches to the *Observer*. "I came straight back here as I felt so upset at home I thought I would rather be on the move," he wrote to Anthony Powell from the Hotel Scribe, only a fortnight after Eileen's death. The most he allowed to show of his inner grief was to call it "a beastly, cruel business."

He had also lost the only person he was prepared to share his work with while it was in progress. "It was a terrible shame that Eileen didn't live to see the publication of *Animal Farm*, which she was particularly fond of and even helped in the planning of," he wrote much later. He read his day's output to her every evening when she got home from the Ministry of Food. According to Lettice Cooper, "She used to come in and tell us next morning how it was getting on. She knew at once it was a winner."

The marriage had not always gone smoothly. Eileen had been a self-sacrificing wife, knowing that Orwell put his work before her, with the necessary egoism of the creative writer. "I was sometimes unfaithful to Eileen and I also treated her very badly," he wrote in a letter of unusual candour. "I think she treated me badly too, at times, but it was a real marriage in the sense that we had been through awful struggles together and she understood all about my work." Besides sharing his struggles, in Spain and in the village store, where she uncomplainingly worked long hours for a profit she estimated at about half-a-crown a week, Eileen came to share his monotone delivery and throwaway style of speech. "It was like listening to his sister talking," David Astor remembers, "You got the impression that they were really related. I think she found Orwell remote in some ways – he could be very off-hand and preoccupied. But when he lost her, it hurt him such a lot that he could never talk about it." "She was the ideal wife for him," said Arthur Koestler, "Matter of fact, practical, brave, warm but not sentimental. She combined the qualities of a hospital nurse and a literary companion."

It was a year before Orwell could bring himself to go back to clear up the cottage they had shared at Wallington. While spending the Christmas of 1945 with Arthur Koestler in Wales, he spoke of his marriage and regretfully referred to "all those things that remain 'unsaid' between two people." Certainly, as far as the rest of the world was concerned, nearly everything remained unsaid.

The reaction that most surprised his friends was Orwell's fierce determination to hang on to their adopted child. As a busy, peripatetic journalist, widowed and in poor health, he had every reasonable excuse for giving up the responsibilities of single parenthood. He would not hear of such a plan. "When I asked him whether he would keep the child," said David Astor, "he practically bit me. 'Of course I will,' he snapped. And he coped with the child heroically." The photographs that exist of George Orwell

Orwell and Richard in Canonbury. "It's like having your childhood all over again," he wrote.

changing his son's trousers, taking him for a walk in his pushchair, or just gazing at him, show tenderness that he rarely displayed openly. A young girl with a child of her own acted as nurse for the boy and housekeeper to Orwell, who was covering the General Election campaign for the *Observer*.

But, naturally, it was a time of great loneliness for Orwell and before long he was proposing marriage – unsuccessfully – to a number of women he knew. One of them was Celia Paget, then 29, whose twin sister, Mamaine, had married Orwell's friend, Arthur Koestler. "Shortly after we met, he invited me round to tea at his flat at Canonbury Square, where he was bathing the baby and putting on his nappy. He was absolutely marvellous with Richard, carrying him about everywhere on his hip. Richard adored him. It was very unusual in those days for fathers to be interested in babies. George was." She discounted his belief that he was unattractive to women: "He was very masculine, huge and yet clever, tender and amusing – you immediately noticed how special he was."

Though the proposal came to nothing, they continued to be close friends and Celia often went round to mind Richard while Orwell went out to engagements. The flat overlooking Canonbury Square was, she remembers, plainly furnished "as if by a working man", with a small room with a workbench where he liked to do carpentry and make toys for Richard. One of the products of his craftsmanship was a curiously shaped homemade armchair. Said one friend, "It was impossible to be comfortable in it in any position." George Woodcock, his anarchist friend, remembered the flat as a dark and dingy place, with shadowy Victorian portraits, sagging homemade bookshelves, china mugs and a screen covered in cut-outs, "a peat fire, black shag tobacco and tea as thick as treacle." There was high tea at 6 o'clock, with kippers. Orwell said it gave you a nice long evening to work in.

This was not the only proposal of marriage that Orwell made in early 1946. Another was to Anne Popham, who was on leave from occupied Germany, sharing a flat in the same house. There was another invitation to tea. But they scarcely knew one another when he proposed by letter soon afterwards. He emphasized to both women what a poor "risk" his health made him at the age of 42, as well as the unlikelihood of his fathering children. "What I am really asking is whether you would like to be the widow of a literary man," he wrote to Anne Popham, with typical ruthlessness and realism. "You are young and healthy and you deserve somebody better than me. On the other hand if you think of yourself as essentially a widow then you might do worse. If I can live another ten years, I think I have another three worthwhile books in me, but I want peace and quiet and someone to be fond of me." And, in a rare and momentary baring of the true state of his inner feelings: "There really isn't anything left in my life except my work and seeing that Richard gets a good start. It is only that I feel so desperately alone sometimes. I have hundreds of friends but no woman who takes an interest in me and can encourage me." Once again, his precipitate attempts to end his loneliness were disappointed.

By then he had taken a decision which made loneliness even more assured. He had paid a visit to the remote island of Jura, off the west coast of Scotland, and determined that he would go up there to live. "Jura was my doing," said David Astor whose family owns a shooting lodge on the island. "In 1945 he was very exhausted, in terrible need of a rest. But he wasn't the sort of person to accept the offer of a comfortable holiday. So I told him I knew of a very remote Scots island with primitive conditions where I thought

Orwell was devoted to Richard. Later it was discovered that he had burned out the name of the natural father on Richard's adoption papers with a lighted cigarette.

Barnhill, Orwell's home on the island of Jura.

a family would take him in. He liked this idea. Then I had to use a lot of persuasion on a neighbouring family. He went up there, thought it the most beautiful place, found an empty farmhouse and immediately started negotiating to rent it. It was the most unsuitable place to go if you were unwell. No telephone. No electricity. One doctor, thirty miles away. A house that had been uninhabited for a long time. The discomfort was unbelievable. The neighbour had to walk eight miles each way to collect bread, milk and meat. One of the attractions to him was the sea fishing."

Another of the attractions to Orwell was the sheer inaccessibility of Jura and of this rather gloomy-looking fortress of a house at the north end of the island (though he described it as "a lovely house"). It was 48 hours from London, involving two separate boat journeys and ending with an eight-mile walk up the track to the house. Before he moved to Jura, he invited V. S. Pritchett to join him in the enterprise, bringing his wife and two young children. Food, he assured him, would be no trouble since there would be fish to catch but, he insisted, they must bring with them their coal ration. "I think he imagined us catching all those boats carrying our belongings and a couple of sacks of coal," Pritchett reflected, "I think he was a man who did very badly want to suffer."

In London, he complained he was "smothered under journalism", producing four articles a week. He was determined to stop all journalism for six months in order to start the novel which had been germinating in his mind since 1943 – the book which was to be

Orwell at his workbench. He liked to do carpentry and make toys for Richard.

Nineteen Eighty-Four. He was also anxious that Richard, a strong, active boy of two, should have the freedom of the countryside in which to run about unconfined by fears of the traffic of Islington.

In May, 1946, he and his surviving sister, Avril, arrived to put the house in order and were joined in July by Richard and his nurse. After three satisfying months of digging a vegetable garden, fishing, putting out lobster pots and shooting rabbits, he began his new novel. He was known on the island as "Mr Blair". The land attached to Barnhill consisted of about 20,000 acres of "heather, bog, peat and snakes", according to Richard Blair's description, "with two or three cows, about twenty sheep, and no end of red deer." To Orwell, that first summer, the island was a place of wild beauty, especially its uninhabited west side, open to the Atlantic. "There are bays of green water so clear that you can see about 20 feet down, with seals swimming about," he wrote. It was the last summer in which he would have health and strength. After the appalling winter of 1946–7, for which he was in London, the remainder of his life on Jura was spent fighting advancing tuberculosis and simultaneously struggling to complete *Nineteen Eighty-Four*.

Before the struggle overwhelmed him to the exclusion of almost all else, Orwell had made his later and most impressive forays in the essay form. The essay on P. G. Wodehouse was the first, and therefore the most badly needed defence of the master over his ill-advised wartime broadcasts from Germany. Orwell had met Wodehouse in Paris in 1945 and realized that he had remained mentally in the Edwardian age and was totally innocent of any desire to collaborate with a real enemy in the real world. To this period belong his important critical essays on Swift's *Gulliver's Travels*, on Tolstoy and Shakespeare, on Salvador Dali, *Such, Such Were the Joys*, and the shudder-making description of his memories of the Paris hospital, *How the Poor Die*; there are amusing trifles such as *Decline of the English Murder* and *Confessions of a Book Reviewer*; above all there is *Politics and the English Language*.

This essay is part of the most valuable legacy that Orwell bequeathed to us. He analyses the use of dead language to defend the indefensible by using such words as "pacification" and "elimination" to describe the killing of defenceless people. What would he have made of the language of nuclear war strategy? He seizes on the most dangerous characteristic of debased ready-made language – it makes clear thinking impossible, especially clear political thinking. Political language, whether that of Conservatives or that of Anarchists, "is designed to make lies sound truthful and murder respectable and to give an appearance of solidity to pure wind." Orwell's rules of thumb for avoiding humbug should be recited by politicians and political writers before they begin any speech or article:

> Never use a metaphor, simile or other figure of speech which you are used to seeing in print; never use a long word where a short one will do; if it is possible to cut a word out always cut it out; never use the passive where you can use the active; never use a foreign phrase, scientific word or jargon word if you can think of an everyday English equivalent.

Orwell's object in framing these rules – with the proviso that it was better to break them than to say something barbarous – was not to improve literary style but to enforce clear speaking. His personal aim was to achieve a style in which it was impossible to utter lies or stupidities without at least making them obvious for what they were.

On his return to Jura in spring, 1947, his progress on the novel was slowed by chest trouble, which he believed had begun in the dreadful fuel-less winter in London, when even Richard's toys were put on the fire to help to keep the room in which Orwell wrote warm. By September, he had decided to stay on the island for the winter, mainly in order to finish the book on schedule. "It's an awful mess at present but I think it has possibilities. I can work quietly here and I think we shall be more comfortable for the winter here than in London," he wrote, "Actually the climate is a bit warmer."

By Christmas, however, he had to go into hospital at East Kilbride, near Glasgow. Doctors diagnosed tuberculosis of the left lung. He admitted in a letter to Julian Symons that he had disregarded his health for the sake of the book. "I thought early in the year that I was seriously ill, but I rather foolishly decided to stave it off for a year as I'd just started a book." As a result he had not been able to do a stroke of work for two or three bedridden months and had lost $1\frac{1}{2}$ stone in weight. But he had finished the first draft, all but the last few hundred words. To his publisher, Warburg, he wrote from hospital: "It's such a ghastly mess as it stands but the idea is so good that I could not possibly abandon it. If anything should happen to me, I've instructed Richard Rees, my literary executor, to destroy the manuscript without showing it to anybody." The world very nearly lost *Nineteen Eighty-Four* then.

Orwell left hospital at the end of July, after six months' inactivity. To the horror of his friends he went straight back to Jura's chilly, damp climate and his book. His lungs soon began to deteriorate again. He did nothing about getting more treatment. He was determined to finish revising the novel first. In September he was halfway through it. In late October he was nearly finished and inquired of his publisher if a typist could be found to come to Jura and type the manuscript under his direction because, unaided, no one could make head or tail of it. "I am rather flinching from the job of typing it. It is a very awkward thing to do in bed, where I have to spend half the time." But despite many efforts, no girl could be found who was prepared to face the journey.

By mid-December, Orwell, propped up on a sofa, had finished typing all 120,000 words of it himself and was totally exhausted, describing himself as "a death's-head". "I am not pleased with the book but I am not absolutely dissatisfied," he wrote to Warburg, "I first thought of it in 1943. I think it is a good idea but the execution would have been better if I had not written it under the influence of TB." To Anthony Powell he even wrote of it as "a good idea ruined." He told Julian Symons: "I ballsed it up rather, partly owing to being so ill while I was writing it."

He was hesitating between two titles, "Nineteen Eighty-Four" and "The Last Man in Europe". Warburg and his colleagues urged him to choose the first. "It is a great book," said Warburg in the report to his colleagues on his first reading of it, "But I pray I may be spared from reading another like it for years to come." Orwell wrote with characteristic pessimism, "It isn't a book I would gamble on for a big sale but I suppose one could be sure of 10,000 anyway." He had already arranged to go into a sanatorium at Cranham, Gloucestershire, immediately after Christmas. "I ought to have done this two months ago but I wanted to get that bloody book finished."

He was never to emerge from hospital again. In that sense he had sacrificed his life to the book, though no one can say how much longer he might have lived, had he not driven and neglected himself as he did. It is sometimes said that Orwell was acting under the compulsion of a death-wish, but there is plenty of evidence that that is nonsense. "Don't think I am making up my mind to peg out," he wrote from Cranham when he was at his

worst, "On the contrary I have the strongest reasons for wanting to stay alive." There were several strong reasons. He wanted to see Richard's boyhood through and give him a start in life. He believed he had more work in him – he was planning a short novel set in 1945, and he began a long short story and essays on Evelyn Waugh and Conrad. When a specialist told him he had a good chance of staying alive if he did no more writing for as much as two years he said he might possibly stick it for one year, but not two. He also had plans to marry Sonia Brownell.

Sonia Brownell, who died in 1980, was *Horizon*'s editorial secretary from 1945 until 1950 when it folded. In effect she was its assistant editor, in the absence of Cyril Connolly or his co-founder, Peter Watson, and her influence on *avant-garde* writers of those years was considerable. Renowned for her beauty – she was once known as "the Euston Road Venus" to the artists of the Euston Road school who painted her portrait – she also had a first-class critical intelligence. She knew everybody in the literary world in London and, later, Paris. Among the writers and painters she befriended were Angus Wilson and Francis Bacon. From the time they met, in 1945, she captivated Orwell, who unsuccessfully proposed to her then as to other women. Later she was to accept him.

Jura has been blamed for Orwell's early death. According to Richard Blair, who grew up on the mainland nearby after Orwell's death, the atmosphere was cold and wet for two days out of three, the house was always cold and the peat they burned gave out little heat. In one way it was typical of Orwell to choose to live in one of the most unsuitable and inaccessible places available in the British Isles. But he did not choose it in a perverse desire to risk his health. The situation appealed to the deepest part of his nature.

No one could have persuaded Orwell to live in a healthier climate or nearer to medical help. No more could anyone have persuaded him to put off writing his last novel. His letters from Jura, when he was not too ill to move out of doors, are the happiest and most optimistic he ever wrote. At last he was alone with Nature, his son and his book. Everything, the seascape, the fishing, the hens and cows and, typically, the very inconveniences and discomforts are enthusiastically detailed. "I am having a splendid time. . . . This is a nice house . . . we are seven miles from anywhere and 25 from a shop . . . however we get plenty of eggs, milk, butter, rabbits and lobsters . . . you'll have to walk the last eight miles, so can you make do with a rucksack?" These are typical snatches from his letters – the outpourings of a happy man.

Another letter speaks laconically of Richard, then three years old, being "wrecked on a desert island and nearly drowned." Richard who, as Orwell hoped, grew up to make a career in farming, remembers the occasion quite vividly. "We had gone round to the west side of Jura one beautiful weekend in a 12-foot dinghy with an outboard motor. On the way back we took the wrong tide, there was a swell and the outboard was flooded and stopped. We rowed to a heather-covered rock that juts out of the water in the Gulf of Corryvrechan, about half a mile from the whirlpool that develops at flood tide. Someone jumped out with a rope, the boat ran up the rock and then was carried out by the running swell and overturned. We were both beneath the boat. George grabbed me, and scrambled ashore." Though Orwell made light of it, it was a dangerous moment, a fight for survival both for the child and for the man with damaged lungs. After spending the afternoon on the rock, they were taken off by a passing lobster boat. The incident rated a paragraph in the *Scottish Daily Express* but as Orwell was known on the island as "Mr Eric Blair" nobody paid attention to it.

Richard's memories of his father are happy ones – of being taken fishing or helping

Sonia Brownell, Orwell's second wife. They met in 1945 and married in 1949, just three months before his death.

about the farm, or of sitting with Orwell eating sweets in their old car which was forever getting punctured on the eight miles of potholed road that led to Barnhill. On one occasion he found an old pipe bowl, filled it with cigarette ends and asked for a light. Orwell greatly amused, passed his lighter and waited philosophically for the boy to be sick.

Once tuberculosis was diagnosed, Orwell worried that Richard had been exposed to possible infection. He got a tuberculin-tested cow to provide the boy with milk and for months at a time had to avoid direct contact with him. He worried equally that their relationship would never develop. "I am afraid of him getting to think of me as just a person who is always lying down and can't play," he wrote from the sanatorium in the last year of his life. Arrangements were made for Richard to spend part of the summer of 1949 nearby in Gloucestershire. He also spent much thought on Richard's education. At first he considered Eton. Eventually he put his name down for Westminster in the hope that he could be a day-boy. Nothing demonstrates more clearly that Orwell did not disassociate himself from his own upbringing and background, as often has been claimed.

The last five years of Orwell's life are full of irony. Fame and fortune had come to him for the first time in 1945, and, at that very moment, he was deprived of the health to enjoy them and of a wife to share them with. He had at last the son he had longed for but was usually not well enough to play with him or to teach him the country pursuits he loved. The idea of fatherhood meant everything to Orwell. When Richard many years later obtained his adoption papers, he discovered that the name of his natural parent was missing from the document. Orwell had burnt it out with a lighted cigarette. He wanted to feel his parenthood was undisputed.

Nineteen Eighty-Four was published on June 6, 1949. Its production was undertaken with as much haste as possible – Warburg seems to have feared that Orwell might not live long enough to read and correct the proofs. The first edition was of 25,000 copies; 22,700 of them had been sold by October, a remarkable figure for a book which is in no sense a typical best-seller and which offers the reader no comfort of any kind. One of the features of the history of the book is its huge and perverse popularity. As a paperback it has sold over ten millions throughout the English-speaking world and exists in twenty-three other languages. When a version of it was performed on television in 1954 it provoked the biggest controversy that the BBC had known up to that time.

It is a tribute to Orwell's imaginative powers that his fantasy found a far wider audience than one purely composed of intellectuals. The book is intended as a warning rather than a prediction. It would not have horrified so many people if they had not inwardly agreed that the terrors described in it were possible, even likely, developments. The title is certainly not meant as a prophecy of how many years it would actually take for Big Brother and the Party to assert total control of every individual. *Nineteen Eighty-Four* is a reversal of 1948 and the feel of that year in Britain; the era of post-war austerity, severe rationing, unrepaired bomb damage, shabbiness, weariness and shortages of such things as razor blades and cigarettes, forms the dingy background of 1984. The dubious synthetic gin of wartime is still on sale. The pinkish-grey stew of the Ministry canteen must have been familiar to Orwell in the BBC canteen. Julian Symons shared five-shilling wartime menus with him in a pub in the Strand and recalls his enthusiasm for the most synthetic dish available – "Victory Pie". He unconsciously remembered it when he imagined Victory gin, Victory cigarettes and Victory "coffee".

Orwell's grave at Sutton Courtenay, Berkshire.

"I don't believe that the kind of society I describe *will* arrive, but I believe something resembling it *could* arrive," wrote Orwell, "Totalitarian ideas have taken root in the minds of intellectuals everywhere and I have tried to draw these ideas out to their logical consequences." A few days after the book was published Orwell felt compelled to state that *Nineteen Eighty-Four* was *not* an attack on Socialism or the British Labour Party, of which he was a supporter.

Perhaps because Orwell's warning is so vivid, it has been effective. Nevertheless, it is worth noticing how near the truth parts of his vision were. The three Superstates of Oceania, Eurasia and Eastasia, dividing the world in a continually shifting balance of power, are there for all to see, though Western Europe, along with Britain (or Airstrip One), is still a satellite of Oceania (the USA) rather than of Eurasia (Soviet Russia). The state of perpetual (non-nuclear) war between the three powers is all too uncomfortably plausible, witness the incessant fighting in one area after another – Vietnam, Cambodia or Afghanistan – in which one or other superpower is engaged. Domestic developments such as the all-seeing, all-hearing "telescreen" seem very close to realization when one considers the closed circuit surveillance of stores and banks and the bugging devices that are used by the police and secret services. And the "two minutes hate" as a form of therapy is virtually an established ritual at football matches, racial demonstrations or in some industrial disputes.

Newspeak can be said to be flourishing in minor ways – words ending in *wise*, for example, enjoyed exactly the vogue Orwell prophesied. Thought is constantly being limited by fashionable jargon words such as "meaningful dialogue" or "perception" which tend to be used to conceal the very lack of meaning, understanding or clear-sightedness that they claim to describe. So far, at least, the habit of altering the truth and tampering with the past is confined to Communist states and Soviet encyclopedias – the sort of thing that made Solzhenitsyn's attempts to establish the truth about the Gulag Archipelago so difficult and heroic. In Britain, *The Times* reposes in its files unaltered – though that, of course, does not prevent politicians denying that their past mistakes occurred or attributing them to each other. There are no Thought Police but Doublethink – "to know and not to know, to be conscious of complete truthfulness while telling carefully constructed lies, to hold simultaneously two opinions which cancel out" – is a well-practised political art. It always was. Lies, connived at by politicians of all parties, attempt to pass into history – they did at the time of Suez and again during the American bombing of Cambodia, to take just two examples. So far, most of them are, with difficulty, eventually uncovered and exposed.

It was the fear that the truth could be buried or cancelled out for ever that haunted Orwell and that comes through the text of *Nineteen Eighty-Four* as perhaps the most heinous crime of all. "If the Party could alter the past and say of this or that event *it never happened* – that surely was more terrifying than torture and death?" One of the weaknesses which Winston noted in Julia is that "she did not feel the abyss opening beneath her feet at the thought of lies becoming truths." Orwell leaves the reader in no doubt that the objective existence of truth and historical fact is the necessary foundation of any kind of social justice. Once the vision of the Party, the collective mind, is accepted without question, reality becomes whatever Big Brother (the ruling oligarchy) cares to make it. The ultimate horror, the negation of all Orwell's values, was enthusiastically to acquiesce, to love Big Brother. If the exposition of the Party philosophy, Ingsoc, by O'Brien seems far fetched and slightly absurd – and it does – if his picture of the future as "a boot stamping on a human face – for ever" seems a piece of inflated rhetoric, then that is because *Nineteen Eighty-Four* has done its immunizing work. It has identified the enemies of humanity. It has given them names and shapes to be watched for and repulsed.

"All writers are vain, selfish and lazy and at the bottom of their motives there lies a mystery. Writing a book is a horrible exhausting struggle, like a long bout of some painful illness." What drives the writer, as Orwell clearly stated in that famous passage from *Why I Write*, is his demon – and in completing "1984" his demon had driven him, as it turned out, to exhaustion. It left him too weak to write anything more of substance except his essay on Gandhi and a last, generous book review – of Churchill's war memoirs. He wrote of Gandhi, whom he did not feel warmly towards, "how clean a smell he has managed to leave behind!" It is an epitaph which he deserved, and would not have disdained, himself.

In September, Orwell was moved from Gloucestershire to University College Hospital in London. On October 13, he was married in a bedside ceremony to Sonia Brownell, whom he had known with an increasing degree of closeness since 1945. David Astor, who was one of the witnesses, recalls it as a slightly macabre but touching ceremony. "I think everybody except George was feeling self-conscious and a bit nervy. It was pretty clear to me that he was dying." Anthony Powell has described the dandyish gesture Orwell made in honour of the occasion. "I really might get some sort of a smoking jacket to wear in bed," he said, "Could you look about and report to me what there is in that line?" A crimson smoking jacket was obtained in time for the wedding which gave Orwell "an unaccustomedly Epicurean air."

At the time of his death, from a haemorrhage on the night of January 21, 1950, aged 46, he thought he had a fair chance of recovery. He was preparing to go to Switzerland with Sonia, to a sanatorium, and he had a fishing rod in his bedroom ready for the trip. "Either I'm better or they don't want a corpse on their hands," he said grimly.

Three days before he died, he made a will in which he made his wife his beneficiary, with provision for Richard's education. He asked to be buried according to the rites of the Church of England, with a plain gravestone inscribed "Here lies Eric Arthur Blair". His other request, that no biography of him should be written, was an impossible hope in view of his subsequent fame and influence. "He believed there is nothing about a writer's life that is relevant to a judgement of his work," said Sonia Orwell. But as the years passed and his stature grew, biographies became inevitable.

Orwell did not die a rich man, nor even a notable best-seller. In 1950 the paperback editions of *Animal Farm* and *Nineteen Eighty-Four* had yet to appear. He was still better known than he was read. "Every writer wants a big seller," he had told Warburg after the success of *Animal Farm*, "It's not so much the money he cares about. A man writes to be read." He never knew – nobody then knew – what a time bomb each of his last two books was to be, how avidly his work was to be read after his death – even the early work that he did not want reprinted. He died dissatisfied with his output, frustrated that for so many years his creativity had been forced into journalism. When, in 1968, the four volume collection of his *Essays, Journalism and Letters* was published, edited by Sonia Orwell and Ian Angus, it was recognized that in Orwell's hands journalism was raised to the level of literature. A column in *Tribune* or a book review was often little, if at all, inferior to his essays, which are considered by many his best work.

In the notebook which he kept in the sanatorium in his last year of life, he reflected on the sixteen years since his first book, *Down and Out*, struggled into print. "Throughout that time there has literally been not one day in which I did not feel that I was idling, that I was behind with the current job, and that my total output was miserably small . . . As soon as a book is finished, I begin, actually from the very next day, worrying because the next one is not begun, and am haunted by the fear that there never will be a next one." Any conscientious writer will recognize this cry with a twinge of sympathetic pain. Orwell's output of nine major books and 700 essays and articles in those sixteen years was almost prolific, given that for so much of the time he was too ill to work. He could see that it was a respectable performance; but this, he wrote, "simply gives me the feeling that I once had an industriousness and a fertility which I have lost."

It is tempting to speculate what he might have written had he lived to see the death, and then the denunciation of Stalin, by which the once-so-unpopular Orwellian view of the tyrant was so triumphantly vindicated. There are those who maintain that Orwell could only thrive in adversity as a minority dissenter. Had he lived on, rich and vindicated, he would have no longer continued to be the scourge of humbug and tyranny. That is a risk that one would willingly have taken. When Dr Johnson died, men felt deprived of a pillar of honest thinking, plain speaking and uncommon sense. It was the same with Orwell. As W. H. Auden put it, "Today, reading his reactions, my first thought is: Oh, how I wish that Orwell were still alive, so that I could read his comments on contemporary events!"

Bibliography

Works by George Orwell with date of first publication

Down and Out in Paris and London	1933
Burmese Days	1934
A Clergyman's Daughter	1935
Keep the Aspidistra Flying	1936
The Road to Wigan Pier	1937
Homage to Catalonia	1938
Coming Up For Air	1939
Inside the Whale and other essays	1940
The Lion and the Unicorn	1941
Animal Farm	1945
Critical Essays	1946
The English People	1947
Nineteen Eighty-Four	1949
Shooting An Elephant and other essays	1950
England Your England and other essays *(Title in U.S.A.: Such, Such Were the Joys)*	1953
Collected Essays	1961
Decline of the English Murder and other essays *(a revised selection)*	1965
The Collected Essays, Journalism and Letters of George Orwell, edited by Sonia Orwell and Ian Angus, 4 Vols	1968

List of Illustrations

79 *The Magnet.* Mrs Stuart Rose.

81 Home Guard, Swiss Cottage. *Local History Collection, Camden Libraries and Arts Department.*

82 London Blitz. *Local History Collection, Camden Libraries and Arts Department.*

84 P. G. Wodehouse. *BBC Hulton Picture Library.*

85 Orwell in Hampstead. *Mrs Mabel Fierz.*

87 Orwell and the BBC Eastern Service, December 1, 1942. *BBC*

89 "As I Please" *From* Tribune, *November 17, 1944.*

90 Aneurin Bevan. *BBC Hulton Picture Library.*

92 Michael Foot by David Low.

National Portrait Gallery.

94 Leon Trotsky at Petrograd Station, March 1920. *BBC Hulton Picture Library.*

95 Nikolai Lenin and Joseph Stalin in the early 1920's. *BBC Hulton Picture Library.*

97 *Animal Farm,* 1st edition, 1945. *Secker & Warburg.*

98 *Animal Farm,* foreign and other editions:
1. Serbo-Croat. *Naprijed, Zagreb/The Orwell Archive.*
2. Swahili. *East African Publishing House, Nairobi/The Orwell Archive.*
3. Polish. *Odnova/The Orwell Archive.*
4. English illustrated edition © *John and Joy Halas.*

99 Animal Farm *in Mauritian Creole.*

O.N.E., Port Louis, Mauritius.

101 Orwell with adopted son, Richard. *From a Private Collection.*

103 Orwell and Richard in Canonbury. *Photo : Vernon Richards.*

105 Orwell and Richard. *Photo : Vernon Richards.*

106 Barnhill, on the island of Jura. *The Orwell Archive.*

107 Orwell at his workbench. *Photo : Vernon Richards/The Orwell Archive.*

110 Sonia Brownell. *The Orwell Archive.*

113 The grave of Eric Arthur Blair at Sutton Courtenay, Berkshire. *Photo : Shearwater Studios.*

Picture research by Illustration Research Service.

Index

Note: Page numbers in *italics* refer to illustrations. GO: George Orwell